SALADS ARE MORE THAN LEAVES.

SALADS ARE MORE THAN LEAVES.

Salads to get excited about

Elena Silcock

hamlyn

First published in Great Britain in 2022 by Hamlyn, an imprint of
Octopus Publishing Group Ltd
Carmelite House
50 Victoria Embankment
London EC4Y 0DZ
www.octopusbooks.co.uk
www.octopusbooksusa.com

An Hachette UK Company
www.hachette.co.uk

Distributed in the US by
Hachette Book Group
1290 Avenue of the Americas
4th and 5th Floors
New York, NY 10104

Distributed in Canada by
Canadian Manda Group
664 Annette St.
Toronto, Ontario, Canada M6S 2C8

Publishing Director: Eleanor Maxfield
Art Director: Yasia Williams
Photographer: Chloe Hardwick
Props Stylist: Daisy Shayler-Webb
Designer: Peter Dawson at gradedesign.com
Assistant Editor: George Brooker
Senior Production Controller: Emily Noto

ISBN 978-0-60063-742-4

A CIP catalogue record for this book is available from the British Library.

Printed and bound in China.

10 9 8 7 6 5 4 3 2 1

Standard level spoon measurement are used in all recipes.
1 tablespoon = one 15ml spoon
1 teaspoon = one 5ml spoon

Contents

Introduction

I've been wanting to write a book about salads since I started writing recipes. Here's the thing: I've always felt like salads never get the limelight they deserve and that they're generally misunderstood. I think many people have a set idea of what a salad is, usually that it's some kind of light lunch or a side to the main event. I reckon it's about time that changed.

Salads can be big and beautiful, they can be a meal in themselves, they can be indulgent, they can be fruity and fresh, they can be full of pasta or they can be a simple assembly of tasty veg. They can be veggie and vegan or they can be a meat feast, and they can be that-dish-that-you-know-will-make-you-look-like-a-chef, upstaging any hunk of meat or fancy fish that dares to show up as an accompaniment to your showstopping salad.

They don't even have to feature leaves at all – I've included a salad here that, in all honesty, is more a kind of cheese plate.

This book is all about redefining salads, making them the starting point of any meal planning, rather than an afterthought when looking for something green to whack on the table. I hope that when you start cooking from this book and see the kind of deliciousness you can label as a salad, you'll jump right on board with the new salad agenda that I've got going on.

HOW TO USE THIS BOOK

I urge you not to skip the next few sections where I try my very best to turn you into a genuine salad maestro. The key is to check out what's good when, because keeping your salads seasonal is the best way to ensure the veg tastes at its very best. The next most important thing is learning to substitute ingredients. I constantly forget items, or rummage through my cupboard *convinced* that I've got a certain spice paste or nut, only to find it's nowhere to be found. Once you know how to easily swap and sub ingredients for what you've got, the number of recipes you can create from this book becomes (almost) endless.

I also cover how to build a salad – a great tool for when you need or want to make a dish from whatever you've got kicking around. It's essentially about working out the layers of flavour and texture that go into creating a salad, ensuring you turn out an epic example every time you go to whip one up.

Finally, I've got a little section on hosting a salad party. I started making two or three salads for friends when they came over, piling the platters in the middle of the table and letting everyone tuck in. It's such a fun way of eating and the book is geared up to make it as easy as possible for you to do the same.

And then there are the recipes themselves, grouped according to their defining characteristic for easy selection, and each feeding four when served on its own, but six as part of a larger meal. I've included an estimated time for how long each salad takes to make, but do note that this is the minimum timing where there are variables or alternative options. Get-ahead tips? Yep, they're in there. Which salads go together well? I've included that in every recipe too. Notes on which salads are for showing off and which are for those looking for something ultra easy – it's all in these pages.

At the end of the day, I'm super-excited for you all to cook up these salads and enjoy them. So go forth and join me in changing up the way salads are perceived, make them the main event and your favourite way to show off your kitchen skills and impress your guests. Prove to everyone that salads really are more than leaves!

WHAT'S GOOD WHEN

Check the date, check the weather, check the mood. Let all those factors have a say in what page you turn to cook from – trust me, once you start working with what's good when, you'll never go back.

Spring

It's the season when I really start to crave fresh flavours, heavy on the greenest of veg and packed with herbs. Try teaming salads with lamb, fresh fish and of course chicken. This is a great time to be cooking the Fitzroy (*see* page 104), Grilled Nutty Greens (*see* page 143) and Spring Veg & Mozzarella (*see* page 197).

What's Good?

Artichokes	Peas
Asparagus	Radishes
Broccoli	Rocket
Chicory	Spring greens
Lettuce	Spring onions
New potatoes	Watercress

Summer

Whatever the weather, summer is the time to cook with alfresco dining in mind. Even when I'm locked up in the rain in the middle of summer, I still prepare salads that make me feel like I could be eating them outdoors in the sunshine! It's time for my favourite tomato salads, Strawberry, Mint & Hazelnut (*see* page 69) and Courgette & Giant Couscous (*see* page 158).

What's Good?

Aubergines	Peppers
Broccoli	Raspberries
Courgettes	Runner beans
Cucumber	Squash
Fennel	Strawberries
Green beans	Sweetcorn
Lettuce	Tomatoes
Mangetout	Wild mushrooms

Autumn

Heading back inside, I'm always looking for something a bit more substantial over autumn. I want to cook with squash and pumpkin all of the time and team my veg up with nutty grains and creamy dressings. My favourite autumn salads are Squash & Freekeh (*see* page 134) and Cauli Wedge (*see* page 139). I'm also obsessed with Pumpkin & Burrata (*see* page 184) for showing off.

What's Good?

Beetroot	Jerusalem artichokes
Brussels sprouts	Parsnips
Cabbage	Pears
Carrots	Potatoes
Cauliflower	Pumpkin
Celeriac	Squash
Chicory	Wild mushrooms

Winter

Winter is a funny salad season because I find it's a halfway house between rich and warm salads packed with roasted veg and creamy cheeses, and the sharp, bitter citrusy salads that feature so heavily on my table during the very short days. Go for the Winter Citrus (*see* page 121), Leeks & Cannelini Beans (*see* page 125) and Carrot, Date & Puy Lentil (*see* page 126).

What's Good?

Apples	Kale
Brussels sprouts	Leeks
Carrots	Oranges
Cauliflower	Parsnips
Celeriac	Pears
Chicory	Squash
Cranberries	Watercress

HOW TO SUB

Throughout the book, I give guidance on what to sub for veggies and vegans. But what about when you forget an ingredient? What about when you can't find it on the shelves of your local supermarket? What if you just don't like it that much? Well, for all of those eventualities, I've got a solution.

Learning to substitute is the key to becoming a better and more confident cook. Knowing how to make a recipe work for the ingredients you've got, or the ingredients you love, makes cooking from cookbooks so much less restrictive, and so much more fun!

The first options to consider are all the dressings and toppers. I've indicated a dressing and topper(s) for each salad in the book, but that's not to say you can't sub in one of the others if you prefer. Fancy croutons rather than roasted nuts? Go for it! Feel like a chilli and lime dressing rather than a lemony olive oil one? Give it a go! I can't promise it'll always work perfectly, but cooking is all about playing with flavours and textures, and hopefully these opening sections will give you the tools to devise new takes on the recipes that follow, as well as totally new salads of your own creation!

Here's a chart of all the different groups of ingredients that I use in the book, and how to interchange them. Will the result be a little different? For sure, but it'll still be delicious, and that's all we're really here for!

INGREDIENT	SUBS
Olive oil	Sunflower, vegetable, rapeseed, sesame or coconut oils – the flavour will change a little, especially if using sesame oil, but they'll all do the trick! You can also swap for butter when you're cooking rather than dressing, but remember that it burns much faster than oil.
Herbs	Sub soft herbs with other soft herbs – these are the likes of flat leaf parsley, coriander, basil and dill. Sub woody herbs with other woody herbs – these include thyme, rosemary and sage. The flavour that these subs provide will be markedly different, but if you know you love the flavour of a particular herb and sub it in, you're not going to be disappointed about what it brings to the party in any case!
Spices	These are a little more tricky, as it's hard to substitute something with such a distinctive flavour with another. Chilli powders or flakes are easier to sub with other hot spices, but when it comes to other sorts of spice, follow your nose. If you don't have some of the spices, you can play around a little and add something else instead – you might create something new and great!
Lemon juice	Swap for lime juice or for a vinegar – you're looking for something that will add a hint of acidity, so use whatever you have.
Vinegar	Vinegars are interchangeable – I use a selection of cider, white wine, red wine, champagne and balsamic. Swap and change, taste and edit your dressing accordingly; balsamic, for example, is sweeter, so you can often skip the sugary element of your dressing if you're using that.

INGREDIENT	SUBS
Spice pastes	Spice pastes such as harissa, Thai red curry and chipotle are very different in flavour and vibe, but they can still be swapped for each other in recipes in order to create something totally new. Try and swap some of the other ingredients if you're working with a whole new spice paste, so that the recipe transforms to stay in keeping with the new flavour profile you're going for.
Lettuce & salad leaves	Swap any lettuce for another, such as Gem for Romaine or oak leaf for Iceberg – they'll all work, but be aware of the way each type behaves when chopped and dressed. For example, a sturdier leaf like Romaine can be swapped for an oak leaf lettuce, but it won't hold that Caesar dressing quite so well. Rocket and watercress can easily be subbed with bags of mixed leaves or lamb's lettuce. The flavours will be much softer when swapping out a peppery leaf, but a lot of people aren't huge fans of peppery leaves and will welcome the swap! Heads of chicory and radicchio or endive are interchangeable but can be hard to get hold of, so they can be swapped for heads of Baby Gem lettuce, though the flavour and texture will be very different.
Green veg	I swap greens in cooking all the time. Use your favourite combos of green beans, asparagus, Tenderstem broccoli, sugar snaps and mangetout, to name a few. Choose what's in season and what looks fresh and delicious when you're shopping.
Onions, shallots & spring onions	Swap for each other or sub in the likes of celery or fennel – all will work perfectly well, but they'll just taste a little different.
Cabbages, broccoli & cauliflower	Swap red cabbage for white cabbage or Hispi cabbage. Broccoli and cauliflower are interchangeable – I've made Raw Broccoli & Almond (see page 33) with cauliflower many times and it's just as delicious. Romanesco cauliflower is a really fun replacement for broccoli if you want to show off a bit!
Root vegetables	Swap carrots, parsnips or even potatoes for each other, or for celeriac, swede, squash or beetroot. The flavours will be different, and some might take a little longer to cook than others, but you can safely make similar recipes with all these ingredients.
Fruit	Fruit can be swapped and varied, but try to keep it in the family – different types of melon can be subbed with each other; swap stone fruit like peaches for other stone fruit such as nectarines or plums; sub apples with pears; and swap oranges for other citrus fruits like clementines, satsumas and grapefruits.
Noodles	All the different noodle types – soba, rice, udon and wheat – can be subbed and swapped, but they all have different cooking times, so be sure to adapt the recipe accordingly.

INGREDIENT	SUBS
Beans, chickpeas & lentils	Swap cans of chickpeas and beans for each other. Lentils and other pulses can also be interchanged, but if cooking from dried, be sure to check cooking times and adapt the recipe accordingly.
Grains & rice	You can interchange different types of rice or grains, but be sure to check the packet for their specific cooking times, as they may vary. For example, if you plan to use brown rice, it takes substantially longer than white rice to cook, so adapt the recipe accordingly.
Pasta	Swap small pasta shapes for others – with the pasta salads in this book, I welcome any small shape! Go for macaroni, farfalle, rigatoni or orecchiette and adjust the cooking times according to the packet instructions.
Yogurt, crème fraîche & soured cream	Sub yogurt with crème fraîche or soured cream and vice versa. I like the lightness that yogurt brings to a dressing, but replacing half with crème fraîche or soured cream will be delicious. I also sub half the yogurt with mayonnaise when dressing potato salad, which makes for a particularly delicious dressing for a tuna salad or a creamy pasta salad too.
Cheeses	I really love to play around with cheeses in salad, and each cheese needs to be treated a bit differently – feta should be crumbled, for example, while Parmesan is for grating or shaving. But regardless, you can swap the cheeses in all of these salads for whichever ones you prefer. I tend to sub like with like, so mild creamy mozzarella with burrata, smelly feta with goats' cheeses and firm, salty Parmesan with pecorino or ricotta salata (salted ricotta). Be experimental, and then use the cheeses that you love the best! But please don't mess around with the Caesar too much (*see* page 164) – I don't want to see that Romaine covered in goats' cheese any time soon!
Cured meats	Swap Parma ham for other cured meats such as bresaola or prosciutto.
Olives, capers & gherkins	When using these ingredients, I'm looking for a sharp, briny flavour that takes a salad from just tasty to super-delicious. These are pretty interchangeable, so you can swap green olives for black or kalamata olives, or capers for chopped gherkins. Feel free to use other briny favourites from your cupboards like pickled chillies.
Nuts & seeds	Nuts and seeds are the most interchangeable of the ingredients I use in this book. I swap and change them in recipes for flavour and to make the salads as varied as possible, but as long as you've got a nutty crunch in there, it's not desperately important which nut or seed you use. What is crucial is always to roast your nuts and toast your seeds. It's not healthier to eat nuts and seeds raw and they sure ain't tastier, so take the time (or buy roasted if you can't spare any) to make sure you get the best from them!

INGREDIENT	SUBS
Dried fruit	Swap sultanas, currants, dried cranberries, dried apricots and dates for each other. Dates are a little trickier to sub because they are so soft, but if you're just chopping them up to throw into the salad, rather than blitzing for a dressing, all of these subs will work perfectly well.

How to Have a Salad Party

I'll admit it might not be the first theme that springs to mind when I say the word 'party', but let me tell you, a salad party is the kind of party that you'll really want to attend.

How does it work?, you ask. Well, basically it consists of choosing two or three salads, whipping them up, and piling them down the middle of a dinner table. It's convivial, it's fun and, mainly, it's seriously delicious. I will allow for the salad party to feature a side – a slow-cooked leg of lamb, some barbecued chicken, maybe a big pot of pasta, for example – but be aware that all eyes ain't gonna be on the accompaniments but looking straight at the salad selection.

I've teamed up the salads, noting on each recipe which salads I think work together best. But feel free to either take my advice or go your own way and compile your own salad guest list. Loads of the salads are designed for mixing and matching, which means you can put together so many different combos that you'll be wanting to invite your friends and family over on repeat just to trial them all.

This is how I go about it. You want to cover your bases: something meaty or cheesy with something fresh and light, and then something a bit more carb heavy. For example, I like to combo the Red Pepper & Bavette (*see* page 159 – meaty), with

The Ultimate Green Salad (*see* page 30 – fresh and light) and the Courgette & Giant Couscous (*see* page 158 – carby). However, you could easily swap in the Triple Tomato (*see* page 44) for The Ultimate Green Salad and the Potato Salad: The Boiled One (*see* page 181) for the Courgette & Giant Couscous. It's also great, and a little less admin heavy, to choose two, then simply toss some greens with a dressing of choice for the side.

Try to work seasonally, and if you're choosing a slightly more high-maintenance salad, go for something a bit simpler to pair with it to save yourself a bit of work! I have included pointers for each recipe on how to get ahead by making dressings, toppers and other elements in advance, leaving you to mainly assemble at the end.

Try to have fun with it – there's something so rewarding about people filling their plates as they pass big and beautiful platters of food around the table. As an added bonus – and to be honest, the main reason I cook for others – people really rave about this kind of eating. I think it's because people don't tend to make incredible salads for themselves, so when they eat vegetables that taste, and look, so delicious, it makes for a memorable meal. That, I guess, is the magic of the salad party.

How to Build a Salad

So you want to make a salad? You've got a refrigerator full of food and want to use it up rather than try to find a recipe that encapsulates all the ingredients you've got on hand. Well, I can help you out with that.

Here's a handy tool that I use when developing salad recipes, which will help you to create your own perfect salad. I like to go through this process before I start so that I know what I'm going to use, and I usually grab all the ingredients and set them out so that I don't forget any. I hope it helps you as much as it helps me!

1. What's your star of the show?

Imagine this as the recipe title: is it a **pumpkin** salad, or is it **roasted carrots**? Is it **red cabbage**, **roasted leeks** or **tomatoes**? Whatever the main veg, that is going to be centre stage of your salad.

2. Extras

Then you probably want a little additional veg, perhaps not the main event but the very important extras, like other roasted veg, cucumber ribbons, sliced radishes, peas or maybe finely sliced green beans. You might also want to add some meat or fish – why not some shredded roasted chicken, cooked peeled prawns or perhaps some cooked and flaked salmon. And my personal favourite – anchovies – get them in there.

3. Leaves

Next, let's talk leaves. Here are some options for you to consider: **rocket, Gem lettuce, kale, chicory, watercress**... the list goes on. On a side note, not all salads need leaves, but if you fancy them, chuck them in!

4. The bulk

Time to make a real meal out of the salad by adding some **drained canned beans** or **chickpeas.** Add a speedy extra by tipping in some **ready-cooked lentils, grains** or **rice.** Or why not try out additions of **torn-up bread** or **cooked and cooled pasta shapes**?

5. Creamy or cheesy

I always think that a salad is improved by some sort of creamy element – this can be a tahini yogurt, a creamy labneh or some sort of cheese. Go for big and soft like a mozzarella or burrata, or ricotta cheese. Go tangy like feta, goats' cheese or a plate covered in thick labneh. Go for firm and grated like a pecorino, Parmesan or ricotta salata (salted ricotta), or go smelly with a Stilton or brie.

6. Herbs

Truly essential. Roughly chop or keep as whole leaves and add to the salad before the final toss. I always reserve a few for the top as well. Go for any combo of **flat leaf parsley, coriander, basil, tarragon, dill** and **mint.** Spice things up by adding **crispy fried sage leaves** or **fried curry leaves** on top.

7. Dressing

When you're making a dressing, there are a few downfalls to be aware of, the most common being not enough oil, not enough salt or not enough acidity. Taste your dressing and then adjust it accordingly. My dressings should work perfectly, but sometimes you may need to add a little more acid or sugar to taste. Take my recipes as guides, but feel free to play with different oils, sources of acidity and extras like toasted spices, sliced fresh chilli and garlic, and capers or olives. When you're making your own dressings, be sure to make a generous amount – no one likes an underdressed salad!

8. Crunch

My personal favourite area. The best bets include toasted nuts and seeds, while shop-bought dukkah and crispy onions and homemade Croutons (see page 23), Savoury Granola (see page 24) and Toasted Breadcrumbs (see page 25) also hit the spot.

Dressings

Dressings

Lemon & Olive Oil

4 tablespoons olive oil
juice of 1–2 lemons, depending on how juicy
    your lemons are (about 2–4 tablespoons) –
    *I tend to start with squeezing 1 juicy lemon,
    taste and add more to taste, squeeze the
    juice of another directly in to the salad
    before serving if needed*
salt and pepper
OPTION: add a pinch of sugar

Put the oil and lemon juice in a large serving or
mixing bowl, season generously with salt and
pepper and whisk until combined. Alternatively,
put the ingredients in a clean jam jar, screw on
the lid tightly and shake well. Store the jar in
the refrigerator for up to a week.

Yogurt

175g (6oz) natural yogurt, or crème fraîche
1 teaspoon clear honey
1 teaspoon Dijon mustard
1 teaspoon cider or white wine vinegar
salt and pepper

Put the yogurt (or crème fraîche), honey,
mustard and vinegar into a mixing bowl,
season generously with salt and pepper and
stir together until combined. Store in an airtight
jar in the refrigerator for up to 2 days.

Honey & Mustard

4 tablespoons olive oil
1–2 tablespoons cider or white wine vinegar
1 teaspoon clear honey
1 teaspoon Dijon mustard
salt and pepper
OPTION: add a grated garlic clove

Put the oil, vinegar, honey and mustard in a
large serving or mixing bowl, season generously
with salt and pepper and whisk until combined.
Alternatively, put the ingredients in a clean jam
jar, screw on the lid tightly and shake well. Store
the jar for up to a week.

Tahini

3 tablespoons tahini
juice of ½ lemon (about 1 tablespoon)
salt and pepper

Put the tahini and lemon juice in a large serving
or mixing bowl, season generously with salt
and pepper and whisk until combined – *it'll
seize up and look clumpy, but don't worry!* Add
splashes of water and keep whisking until it
becomes a light creamy colour and a drizzling
consistency – *it can take up to 5 tablespoons
water, so have no fears about it continuing to
look clumpy for a while!* Store in an airtight jar
in the refrigerator for up to a week.

Green Sauce

50g (1¾oz) soft herbs – *you can use any kind, such as flat leaf parsley, coriander, mint, basil, dill, tarragon or chives*

5 tablespoons olive oil, or more if needed

juice of 1 lemon (about 2 tablespoons)

pinch of sugar

salt and pepper

Pull the herb leaves from the stems and put into a mini chopper or blender (*but feel free to throw in any coriander and parsley stems*), add the oil, lemon juice and sugar and season generously with salt and pepper. Blitz into a smooth sauce, adding a little more oil if it's a bit too thick. Store in an airtight jar in the refrigerator for up to 3 days, but be aware that the herbs will turn brown if not used on the day it's made.

Top tip: if you want your green sauce to be *extra* green, finely chop the herbs, then simply mix them with the oil, lemon juice and sugar. This is a bit of a cheffy trick, not necessary for a delicious-tasting sauce but a fun way to show off a little in the kitchen!

Make it salsa verde: Throw in a 50g (1¾oz) can of anchovy fillets in olive oil, oil and all, with 2 tablespoons capers and 1 teaspoon Dijon mustard before blitzing the sauce until smooth.

Make it a zhoug: Heat a dry frying pan over a medium-high heat, add 1 teaspoon each coriander seeds, cumin seeds and fennel seeds and toast for about a minute until fragrant. Crush with a pestle and mortar and stir through the blitzed sauce.

Make it vegan avo dressing: Add 1 peeled and stoned avocado before blitzing the sauce until smooth.

Caesar

1 fresh egg yolk

½ × 50g (1¾oz) can of anchovy fillets in olive oil, drained but reserving a splash of the oil

juice of ½ lemon (about 1 tablespoon), or more to taste

1 teaspoon Dijon mustard, or more to taste

1 garlic clove, peeled (optional)

75ml (5 tablespoons) olive oil

splash of Worcestershire sauce

40g (1½oz) Parmesan cheese, finely grated

salt and pepper

Put the yolk into a mini chopper or blender, add the anchovies, lemon juice, mustard and garlic clove, if using, and blitz to a paste. You can also do this by finely chopping the anchovies and finely grating in the garlic, then whisking them up with the egg yolks, lemon juice and mustard. Add the splash of anchovy oil and blitz again — or whisk if making by hand. Then with the machine running, pour in the olive oil in a very slow and steady stream until the mixture has emulsified into a thick dressing. If using a whisk, simply keep whisking as you add the oil a little at a time. Add a splash of water if it starts to look greasy. Once all the oil has been incorporated, add a large pinch of salt and pepper, then taste and season with more lemon juice and mustard, if you like, and the Worcestershire sauce to taste. Stir in the Parmesan and then add a little water if it's too thick — it should be the consistency of double cream. Store in an airtight jar in the refrigerator for up to 3 days.

Make a cheat's Caesar: If whisking up the yolk and oil scares you a bit, simply make this cheat's version instead. Put 75g (2¾oz) mayonnaise in a mixing bowl and finely grate or crush in a garlic clove. Add 1 teaspoon Dijon mustard and a squeeze of lemon juice. Drain ½ × 50g (1¾oz) can of anchovy fillets in olive oil, reserving a splash of the oil, and finely chop, then stir through the mayo along with the anchovy oil and 40g (1½oz) finely grated Parmesan cheese. Season well with salt and pepper and add a splash of water to loosen to the consistency of double cream. Store as for the Caesar.

Miso & Lime

1 tablespoon miso paste
juice of 2 limes (about 2 tablespoons) or
   2 tablespoons rice wine vinegar
1 teaspoon clear honey
3 tablespoons sesame oil
salt and pepper

Whisk the miso paste with the lime juice in a large serving or mixing bowl to loosen it. Add the honey and sesame oil, season generously with salt and pepper and whisk until combined. Alternatively, put the ingredients in a clean jam jar, screw the lid on tightly and shake well. Store in an airtight jar in the refrigerator for up to a week.

Chilli & Lime

1 tablespoon chilli sauce – *I use Sriracha*
juice of 1–2 limes, depending on how juicy
   they are (about 1–2 tablespoons)
4 tablespoons oil – *I use a mixture of sesame
   oil and sunflower or vegetable oil*
1 tablespoon soy sauce
1 teaspoon sugar
salt and pepper

Put the chilli sauce, lime juice, oil, soy sauce and sugar into a large serving or mixing bowl, season generously with salt and pepper and whisk until combined. Alternatively, put the ingredients in a clean jam jar, screw the lid on tightly and shake well. Store in an airtight jar in the refrigerator for up to a week.

Anchovy & Lemon

50g (1¾oz) can of anchovy fillets in olive oil
2 garlic cloves, peeled
4 tablespoons olive oil
½ small bunch (about 15g/½oz) flat leaf parsley
finely grated zest and juice of 1 lemon
salt and pepper

Put the anchovies, including the oil from the tin, in a small saucepan. Grate the garlic directly into the pan. Add the olive oil and cook over a low heat for 10 minutes, stirring regularly, and pressing the anchovies until they have melted into a paste. Remove from the heat and set aside to cool a little. Pull the parsley leaves from the stems and finely chop, then add to the pan along with the lemon zest and juice. Taste and season with salt and pepper. Store in an airtight jar in the refrigerator for up to 3 days, but be aware that the parsley will turn brown if not used on the day it's made.

Toppers

Toppers

I often add some of these toppers to a salad as I'm tossing it, and when I do this, I've included them in the ingredients list so that you can be sure they're not optional. The croutons in both the Peach Panzanella (*see* page 55) and Winter Panzanella (*see* page 116), for example, are not up for debate. In most instances, the roasted nuts are not really optional, so they often make their way into the ingredients lists as well. Some of the others, the more fancy options like the Savoury Granola, are great for having around to top any of your salads. I want this book to inspire you to make up your own salads and to use the toppers to your liking!

Herbs

I almost always top my salads with herbs, but they are always in the salad itself, so I just hold a few back and sprinkle them over at the end. I'd like to say that this is for flavour, but in all honesty it's just because salads (and maybe most foods) look so much more appetizing when finished with some fresh herbs.

Roasting Nuts & Toasting Seeds to Perfection

I always roast nuts in a big batch rather than just enough for a single salad, as I'm a fiend for them and know they'll get eaten within a few days. You can of course buy nuts ready roasted – *I always use roasted and salted peanuts* – but in my experience other roasted nuts are often harder to find and they're usually not roasted enough for me, so that's when the home roasting really comes in handy!

Make sure you use unroasted nuts, and if using hazelnuts, go for the blanched kind.

Preheat the oven to 180°C/160°C fan/350°F/Gas Mark 4. Spread the nuts out in a roasting tray – you can add as many nuts of all different types (except pine nuts; *see* below) as you like so long as they aren't too deep in the tray – *I roast up to 500g/1lb 2oz at a time.* Roast for 15–20 minutes until golden – *cooking the nuts at a relatively low temperature means they become golden and sweet rather than risking them turning dark and bitter tasting.* Pine nuts are a bit of an exception to the rule. Roast in the same way but for 10 minutes only until golden – *keep your eyes on them, as they can turn from golden to dark and bitter very fast!* Set the roasted nuts aside to cool, then store in an airtight container for up to 2 months.

Make spiced nuts: Toss 200g (7oz) hot freshly roasted nuts in 15g (½oz) butter, 1 teaspoon brown sugar, 1 teaspoon smoked paprika and 1 teaspoon finely chopped rosemary or thyme leaves. Season with salt and pepper, then spread out on nonstick baking paper to cool completely.

Toast your seeds: Add whichever seeds you're using to a dry frying pan, then place over a medium heat and toast for 2–4 minutes, depending on the type/size of the seeds, tossing regularly – *with most seeds, they'll start to pop once they're ready.* Set aside to cool. Store in an airtight container for up to 2 months.

Toppers to Buy

Chilli flakes – I love to use Aleppo pepper (pul biber)
Crispy onions
Crunchy corn
Dukkah
Roasted, salted peanuts
Smoked almonds
Tortilla chips

How to Quick Pickle Anything* You Fancy

*I say *anything*, but that might be a bit of an overstatement, as this method is best suited to raw vegetables. Experiment with your favourites and feel free to add extras like lemon zest or spice seeds. A few of my recipes call for pickles on top, and I often pickle the ingredients in the dressing while I make the rest of the salad, but if you want to add pickles as an additional topping, follow these super-simple steps. I recommend chucking in a bit of the pickling liquor when you toss the salad!

100g (3½oz) raw vegetables, finely sliced – try red onion, radishes, carrots, Tenderstem broccoli stems, asparagus spears etc. 100ml (3½fl oz) red or white wine vinegar or cider vinegar 1 teaspoon salt 1 teaspoon sugar	Put the raw veggies into a mixing bowl and add a splash of boiling water to soften them slightly, then add the remaining ingredients and stir well. Set aside for 10–15 minutes for a light pickling. Store in an airtight container in the refrigerator – quick-pickled onions or shallots will only last a couple of weeks, but other veg will keep for up to a month.

Croutons

250g (9oz) bread, torn into 2–3cm (¾–1¼-inch) chunks – *I like to use sourdough* 2 tablespoons olive oil salt	Preheat the oven to 180°C/160°C fan/350°F/Gas Mark 4. Spread the croutons out in a roasting tray, drizzle with the oil and season generously with salt. Toss well, making sure that the croutons are well coated with the oil. Roast for 10–15 minutes, until the garlic is golden and crisp. Set aside to cool before using.
Make fennel croutons: add 1 tablespoon of fennel seeds to the croutons with the salt.	**Make garlic 'n' herb croutons:** add 2 grated garlic cloves and 1 tablespoon finely chopped flat leaf parsley leaves or dried oregano to the croutons after drizzling with the oil and seasoning with salt.

Crispy Chickpeas

400g (14oz) can of chickpeas
1½ tablespoons olive oil
salt
OPTION: add 2 teaspoons of any ground
   spices such as curry powder, ground
   coriander, ground cumin or smoked paprika
   to make a spiced version

Preheat the oven to 180°C/160°C fan/350°F/
Gas Mark 4. Line a baking tray with nonstick
baking paper. Drain and rinse the chickpeas,
then drain well and pat them dry with kitchen
paper. Spread out on the lined tray and add the
oil. Sprinkle with the spices, if using, season
generously with salt and toss well. Roast for
20–30 minutes, shaking the pan every 10
minutes, until golden and crispy. Be careful
and stand back when shaking the pan, as
sometimes they can pop open in the oven.
Set aside to cool. Loosely cover and use within
2 days. If they go soft, put them back in a hot
oven to crisp up again.

Savoury Granola

100g (3½oz) jumbo oats
100g (3½oz) nuts, roughly chopped – *I use
   blanched hazelnuts, almonds (with their
   skins on or blanched) or walnuts*
3 tablespoons seeds – *I use sesame and
   pumpkin*
3 tablespoons olive oil
1 tablespoon maple syrup
1 tablespoon soy sauce
1 egg white, lightly beaten
salt
OPTION: add 2 teaspoons fennel seeds,
   2 teaspoons cumin seeds and 1 teaspoon
   smoked paprika to make a spiced version

Preheat the oven to 180°C/160°C fan/350°F/Gas
Mark 4. Line a baking tray with nonstick baking
paper. Toss all the ingredients together in a bowl
along with a big pinch of salt, then spread out
on the lined tray. Toast for 30–40 minutes until
golden and crisp. Set aside to cool. Store in an
airtight container for up to 2 months.

Crispy Capers

Place a saucepan over a medium-high heat, add enough vegetable or sunflower
oil to come about 2cm (¾ inch) up the side of the pan and heat until shimmering
(180°C/350°F). Line a plate with kitchen paper, and have a lid at the ready! Drain
the capers really well and pat dry with kitchen paper, then add to the hot oil –
*STAND BACK, as they can spit a little, shielding yourself from the spitting with
the pan lid if necessary!* Fry for 2–3 minutes until the capers are crispy and their
shells have flared out a little. Use a slotted spoon to remove and transfer to the
lined plate to drain. Once cool, store in an airtight container for up to 2 days
(beyond that they'll start to soften).

Pitta Chips

3 pitta breads
2 tablespoons olive oil
salt
OPTION: add 1 tablespoon za'atar

Preheat the oven to 180°C/160°C fan/350°F/
Gas Mark 4. Cut the pittas in half, as if you
were splitting them open to fill. Cut each half
into triangles and spread out in a roasting tray.
Drizzle with the oil and season generously with
salt. Sprinkle with the za'atar, if using. Toss well,
making sure that the pitta chips are well coated
with the oil. Roast for 10–15 minutes, shaking
the pan every 5 minutes, until golden and
crunchy. Set aside to cool. Store in an airtight
container for up to 2 weeks

Chilli Oil

Always welcome to push a salad from tasty to
unbelievably good, this makes a great addition
to dressings, or just for drizzling on at the end!

75ml (5 tablespoons) vegetable or sunflower oil
1 red chilli, finely sliced
1 tablespoon chilli flakes
2 garlic cloves, finely sliced
knob of fresh root ginger, peeled and finely
    sliced into matchsticks
1½ tablespoons sesame seeds
1 teaspoon crushed Sichuan peppercorns
    (optional)

Put all the ingredients in a small saucepan.
Place over a low heat and cook for 10–15
minutes until the garlic is golden and crisp.
Set aside to cool before using.

Toasted Breadcrumbs

100g (3½oz) fresh breadcrumbs
1 garlic clove, grated
2 tablespoons olive oil
finely grated zest of 1 lemon
salt
Make them spicy: add a pinch of chilli powder,
    smoked paprika or curry powder
Make them herby: add 1 tablespoon
    finely chopped flat leaf parsley, mint or
    coriander leaves
Make them nutty: Swap 4 tablespoons of the
    breadcrumbs for 4 tablespoons desiccated
    coconut or ground almonds

Toss the breadcrumbs (and coconut or ground
almonds, if using) with the garlic and oil in a
bowl. Add the ground spices, if using, and
season well with salt. Put the breadcrumb
mixture in a frying pan and fry over a medium
heat for 6–8 minutes until golden. Meanwhile,
add the lemon zest, and herbs if using, to
the bowl and line a plate with kitchen paper.
Transfer the toasted breadcrumbs to the lined
plate to drain, then add to the lemon zest and
herbs, if using, and toss well. Once cool, store
in an airtight container for up to 2 days.

Fresh

'The next few pages are full of the recipes I like to make when I'm really in the mood for a salad salad – something a bit light, zesty and crunchy. Don't be fooled, they're not diet salads, they've got all the goods, but they're packed with raw leaves and veg and never fail to hit the spot.'

Courgette & White Bean

SERVES 4
TIME 20 mins
VIBE Easy-peasy

NICE ON THE SIDE
Chicken or fish

SALAD PARTY?
Serve with The Ultimate Green Salad (*see* page 30) and/or Prawn Cocktail (*see* page 175)

1 tablespoon fennel seeds
50g (1¾oz) pistachio nuts
2 courgettes
2 celery sticks
120g (4¼oz) pitted green olives
2 × 400g (14oz) cans white beans – *cannellini, haricot or butter*
large handful of mixed herbs – *I used dill and flat leaf parsley*
75g (2¾oz) Parmesan cheese
salt and pepper

DRESSING
Honey & Mustard (*see* page 16)

TOPPERS
a little of the Parmesan (*see above*)
a few of the pistachio nuts (*see above*)

Photographed on page 26

Raw courgettes used to feel like a weird choice to me, and don't get me wrong, charred courgettes are incredible (*see* my Lamb Meatballs with Charred Courgettes on page 150 and Courgette & Giant Couscous on page 158). But there is something so fresh about raw courgettes and the way they taste when drenched in a delicious dressing.

SUBS Ⓥ Use a vegetarian hard cheese. ⓥ Use vegan Parmesan-style 'cheese' and swap the honey in the dressing for sugar or maple syrup.

GET AHEAD Make the dressing, including toasting the fennel seeds, and roast the pistachios in advance.

1] Whisk up the dressing in a large mixing bowl. Heat a dry frying pan over a medium-high heat, add the fennel seeds and toast for about a minute until fragrant. Add to the dressing.

2] Roast the pistachios (*see* page 22). Meanwhile, slice the courgettes into discs 3mm (⅛ inch) thick, finely slice the celery and slice the olives, then add to the bowl. Drain and rinse the beans, then drain well and add to the bowl.

3] Pull the herb leaves from the stems and add to the salad. Use a peeler to shave most of the Parmesan directly into the bowl. Roughly chop the toasted nuts and add most of them to the bowl. Toss, taste and season with salt and pepper. Transfer to a platter, then shave over the remaining Parmesan and sprinkle over the remaining nuts.

Frozen Pea, Mint & Cucumber

SERVES 4
TIME 30 mins
VIBE Easy-peasy

NICE ON THE SIDE
Chicken, fish, sausages or slow-cooked lamb shoulder

SALAD PARTY?
Serve with Triple Tomato (*see* page 44) and/or Egg, Bacon & Gem Lettuce (*see* page 169)

200g (7oz) couscous
200ml (7fl oz) boiling water
1 jalapeño or other medium hot green chilli
175g (6oz) frozen peas
1 small cucumber
1 small bunch (about 30g/1oz) mint
1 small bunch (about 30g/1oz) coriander
200g (7oz) block feta cheese
salt and pepper

DRESSING

Honey & Mustard (*see* page 16), plus 1 extra tablespoon vinegar, or more to taste

TOPPERS

75g (2¾oz) walnuts or blanched hazelnuts
a few of the herbs (*see* above)

Using frozen peas in salad was a bit of a revelation to me. They defrost as you toss the salad, but they also keep everything cold and fresh.

SUBS 🆅 Swap the honey in the dressing for sugar or maple syrup and the feta for firm tofu.

GET AHEAD Make the couscous up to 24 hours in advance and set aside to cool completely, then toss with the peas and store in an airtight container in the refrigerator. Roast the nuts in advance.

1] Put the couscous into a bowl with a pinch of salt. Pour over the measured boiling water, cover with clingfilm and leave to sit for 10 minutes. Remove the clingfilm, fluff up the couscous with a fork and then leave for 10–15 minutes to cool to room temperature.

2] Meanwhile, whisk up the dressing including the extra tablespoon of vinegar in a large mixing bowl. Finely slice the chilli, add to the dressing and set aside. Roast the nuts (*see* page 22).

3] Add the peas to the chilli in the bowl and top with the couscous – *the residual heat will defrost the peas*. Chop the cucumber into 1cm (½-inch) chunks and add to the bowl. Pull the herb leaves from the stems, roughly chop and add most to the bowl. Toss, taste and season generously with salt and pepper, adding more vinegar to taste. Add the feta, crumbling it into chunks with your hands, and gently toss again – *you don't want to break up the feta too much!* Top with the remaining herbs. Roughly chop the roasted nuts and sprinkle on top.

The Ultimate Green Salad

SERVES 4
TIME 15 mins
VIBE Easy-peasy

NICE ON THE SIDE
Chicken, fish, slow-cooked meats or creamy pastas – I serve this salad with pretty much everything

SALAD PARTY?
Serve with Courgette & White Bean (*see* page 28) and/or Triple Tomato (*see* page 44)

2 shallots or 1 onion
190g (6¾oz) jar of gherkins
juice of 1 lemon (about 2 tablespoons)
½ iceberg lettuce – *straight from the refrigerator*
2 Gem lettuces – *straight from the refrigerator*
2 large handfuls of soft herbs (optional) – *I use a mixture of flat leaf parsley and dill*

DRESSING
Honey & Mustard (*see* page 16)

I know, salads are more than leaves, but also sometimes a leafy salad, a really, really great leafy salad is what's needed. This one is packed with crunchy lettuce, leafy greens and herbs and tossed in a sharp dressing. Oh – and the gherkins – the best addition to a green salad I've ever made.

SUBS Ⓥ Swap the honey in the dressing for sugar or maple syrup.

GET AHEAD Prepare everything a few hours in advance. Pile the lettuces and herbs into the bowl BUT do not toss. Cover and store in the refrigerator. Remove and toss to serve.

1] Whisk up the dressing in a large serving bowl. Peel and finely chop the shallots or onion, then add to the bowl. Drain and slice the gherkins, then add these to the bowl too. Add the lemon juice and toss to combine. Set aside until needed.

2] Shred your lettuces – you can either finely slice them or cut into 2.5cm (1-inch) slices like I prefer to. *If your lettuces look at all dirty, wash in iced water and spin to dry.* Add the lettuces to the salad dressing along with the herbs and mixed greens, if using, toss and serve immediately.

Poached Ginger Chicken

SERVES 4
TIME 30 mins, plus cooling
VIBE Not too tricky

NICE ON THE SIDE
Fried greens, fried rice or prawn crackers

SALAD PARTY?
Serve with Tomatoes With Chilli Oil (*see* page 72) and/or Spicy Noodle (*see* page 79)

thumb-sized chunk of fresh root ginger, sliced

1 chicken stock cube

3 skinless chicken breasts

1 bunch (about 200g/7oz) radishes

1 bunch (about 100g/3½oz) spring onions

200g (7oz) sugar snap peas

3 carrots

½ red cabbage (about 350g/12oz)

1 small bunch (about 30g/1oz) coriander

75g (2¾oz) roasted, salted peanuts

salt and pepper

DRESSING

2 batches Miso & Lime (*see* page 19)

TOPPERS

a few of the coriander leaves

a few of the peanuts (*see* above)

Poaching and shredding chicken has been an art that I've really tried to master: too much and it's dry and chewy; too little and you're playing with fire. But I think it's finally on point here! Don't skimp on the dressing – all that red cabbage needs it!

SUBS Ⓥ Ⓥ Swap the poached chicken for marinated firm tofu.

GET AHEAD Cook and shred the chicken up to 3 days in advance, then store in an airtight container in the refrigerator. Make the dressing in advance.

1] Put the ginger and stock cube in a large pan of water, place over a high heat and bring to the boil, stirring to dissolve the stock cube. Once at a rolling boil, add the chicken breasts, bring back to the boil – *the heat will drop when you add the chicken* – then remove from the heat and set aside for 20 minutes.

2] Meanwhile, whisk up the dressing in a mixing bowl. Finely slice the radishes and finely shred the cabbage, and add both to the dressing and set aside.

3] Remove the chicken from the poaching liquid and set aside on a plate to cool. Once cool, shred the chicken on to a plate, cover with clingfilm and set aside in the refrigerator until ready to assemble the salad.

4] Finely slice the spring onions and sugar snaps on the diagonal and put them in a large mixing bowl. Peel the carrots, then use the peeler to peel them into ribbons directly into the bowl. Pull the coriander leaves from the stems and add most of them to the bowl along with most of the peanuts.

5] Add the shredded chicken and dressing to the salad. Toss to combine, taste and season with salt and pepper. Transfer to a platter or plates and top with the remaining coriander leaves and peanuts.

Raw Broccoli & Almond

SERVES 4
TIME 30 mins
VIBE Easy-peasy

NICE ON THE SIDE
Roasted feta cheese,
roast chicken, tomato pastas or fish

SALAD PARTY?
Serve with Creamy Pasta (*see* page 167) and/or Spring Veg & Mozzarella (*see* page 197)

1 large head of broccoli (about 325g/11½oz)

2 lemons

3 tablespoons olive oil

100g (3½oz) almonds

200g (7oz) green beans

120g (4¼oz) rocket

60g (2¼oz) Parmesan cheese

50g (1¾oz) mixed soft herbs – *I used flat leaf parsley and chives*

salt and pepper

DRESSING

Yogurt (*see* page 16)

TOPPERS

a few of the herbs (*see* above)

a few of the almonds (*see* above)

Raw broccoli is a powerhouse salad ingredient, and covering it in yogurt dressing makes for a match made in heaven.

SUBS Ⓥ Use a vegetarian hard cheese. Ⓥ Use vegan Parmesan-style 'cheese', and vegan yogurt subbed for dairy yogurt and maple syrup instead of honey in the dressing.

GET AHEAD Roast the almonds and make the dressing in advance.

1] Stand the broccoli head upside down on a chopping board. Use a knife to slice down around the head, shaving off small chunks of the broccoli florets as you go. *This is the easiest method to chop it as finely as possible.* Put in a large mixing bowl. Finely slice the broccoli stalk and add to the bowl. Finely grate in the zest of one of the lemons and squeeze in the juice, then add the oil and a big pinch of salt. Use your hands to massage the dressing into broccoli, then set aside to marinate a little while you make the rest of the salad.

2] Roast the almonds (*see* page 22). Mix up the dressing.

3] Cut the green beans into 2cm (¾-inch) lengths and add to the bowl with the broccoli, then add the rocket. Roughly chop the roasted almonds and add most of them to the bowl. Use a fine grater or Microplane to grate the Parmesan directly into the bowl. Slice or snip the chives, if using. Pull the parsley or other herb leaves from the stems and roughly chop. Add most of the herbs to the bowl. Toss, taste and add the juice of the second lemon if it needs it – *if not, cut into wedges to serve* – along with some pepper. Transfer to a platter or bowls. Drizzle with the yogurt dressing and top with the remaining herbs and roasted almonds.

A Kinda Niçoise

SERVES 4
TIME 30 mins, plus cooking
VIBE Not too tricky

NICE ON THE SIDE
A big baguette and a lot of salted butter!

SALAD PARTY?
Serve with Charred Lettuce (*see* page 153) and/or Spring Veg & Mozzarella (*see* page 197)

750g (1lb 10oz) new potatoes
4 eggs
200g (7oz) green beans
1 red onion
2 × 145g (5oz) cans of tuna in olive oil – *get the best quality you can*
60g (2¼oz) capers
85g (3oz) pitted black olives
salt and pepper
mayonnaise, to serve (optional)

DRESSING
Lemon & Olive Oil (*see* page 16) or Anchovy & Lemon (*see* page 19)

TOPPERS
50g (1¾oz) almonds or 30g (1oz) pine nuts
a few flat leaf parsley leaves

If you have the time, I really recommend taking the slightly more long-winded approach here and making your own tuna in olive oil, but otherwise get a very good can of tuna – when it's the star of the salad, you want it to taste as good as possible. The mayo is optional, but honestly, I think you should make it compulsory.

SUBS Ⓥ ⓋⒻ Swap the tuna for chickpeas or marinated firm tofu, and use vegan mayonnaise to serve for vegans or omit. Omit the egg.

GET AHEAD Make the dressing and roast the nuts in advance.

1] Make the dressing and set aside. Roast the almonds or pine nuts (*see* page 22).

2] Scrub the potatoes if dirty, then halve any larger ones. Put into a large saucepan, cover with water and add a big pinch of salt. Place over a high heat and bring to the boil. Meanwhile, fill a bowl with iced water. Once the potatoes are boiling, set a timer for 20 minutes. After 13 minutes, add the eggs, and after 17½ minutes, add the green beans. Once the timer goes off, use a slotted spoon or tongs to remove the eggs and add to the iced water, then drain the potatoes and green beans and add them too.

3] Peel and finely slice the red onion. Line a plate with kitchen paper, then remove the potatoes and green beans from the iced water on to the lined plate to dry. Shell the eggs.

4] To serve, halve the eggs and add 2 halves to each plate. Drain the tuna and add to the plates. Pile the beans, potatoes and red onion around the plates. Top with the capers and olives, then drizzle over the dressing. Finish with the roasted almonds or pine nuts, parsley leaves and a big crack of black pepper. I like to serve with a dollop of mayo.

Tabbouleh

SERVES 4
TIME 30 mins
VIBE Easy-peasy

NICE ON THE SIDE
Roast chicken, grilled aubergines or hummus and falafel

SALAD PARTY?
Serve with Spicy Steak (*see* page 76) and/or Cauli Wedge (*see* page 139)

2 teaspoons Lebanese seven-spice mix
1 red onion
6 tomatoes
200g (7oz) bulgur wheat
50g (1¾oz) flat leaf parsley
50g (1¾oz) mint
4 spring onions
salt and pepper

DRESSING
Lemon & Olive Oil (*see* page 16), plus the juice of 1 extra lemon (about 2 tablespoons)

TOPPERS
Crispy Chickpeas (*see* page 24), optional

I had to include a tabbouleh in this book. I love it. It can take a bit of herb-chopping practice, but trying not to over-chop your herbs does makes all the difference to the zingy freshness of this salad. If you can't find Lebanese seven-spice mix, use a mixture of ground cinnamon and allspice.

GET AHEAD Make the dressing and crispy chickpeas in advance. Cook the bulgur wheat up to 2 days in advance and store in an airtight container in the refrigerator.

1] Whisk up the dressing including the extra lemon juice in a mixing bowl. Stir in the seven-spice mix. Peel and finely slice the red onion, then add to the dressing and set aside.

2] Finely chop the tomatoes, add to a seperate large mixing bowl with a big pinch of salt and set aside.

3] Bring a pan of salted water to the boil. Add the bulgur wheat and simmer over a medium-high heat for 7–10 minutes until cooked through.

4] Drain the bulgur in a sieve and rinse with cold water until completely cooled. Set aside in the sieve over a bowl to drain completely.

5] Drain off any liquid from the tomatoes in the bowl – *salting and draining the tomatoes intensifies their flavour*. Working with each bunch of herbs in turn, hold the stems and run a knife through the leaves – *you want to finely shred the leaves, but not over-chop them so that they stay fresh and unbruised!* Add the herbs to the bowl of tomatoes.

6] Finely slice the spring onions and add to the bowl. Add the bulgur wheat and the dressing and red onion, then season generously with salt and pepper and toss well. Spoon the tabbouleh into bowls and top with crispy chickpeas, if using.

Miso Noodle, Avo & Cucumber

SERVES 4
TIME 15 mins
VIBE Not too tricky

NICE ON THE SIDE
Soy chicken wings or spiced pork ribs

SALAD PARTY?
Serve with Poached Ginger Chicken (*see* page 32) and/or Thai Red Aubergine (*see* page 86)

400g (14oz) soba noodles

250g (9oz) frozen edamame beans

2 avocados

1 large cucumber

1 small bunch (about 30g/1oz) coriander

2–3 tablespoons soy sauce

salt and pepper

lime wedges, to serve

Sriracha, to serve

DRESSING

Miso & Lime (*see* page 19), plus 2 tablespoons tahini

TOPPERS

30g (1oz) sesame seeds

a few of the coriander leaves (see above)

pinch of chilli flakes

I make a version of this salad about once a week. It's speedy, it's fresh and I'm a sucker for the tahini dressing, which I highly recommend making extra of, ready to toss over any veg you cook over the next few days.

GET AHEAD Cook the noodles up to 1–2 days in advance and leave in iced water *so that they don't stick together*, then drain, toss in a little sesame oil and store in an airtight container in the refrigerator. Toast the sesame seeds and make the dressing in advance.

1] Bring a large pan of salted water to the boil, add the soba noodles and cook according to the packet instructions. Fill a bowl with iced water and add the edamame beans. Once the noodles are cooked, drain in a sieve, rinse with cold water and add to the bowl of iced water and edamame beans. Set aside.

2] Toast the sesame seeds (see page 22). Whisk up the dressing including the tahini in a large mixing bowl, adding a splash of water to make it a drizzling consistency. Halve each avocado and remove the stone, then peel and cut into 1cm (½-inch) cubes. Add to the dressing. Cut the cucumber in half lengthways, then use a spoon to scrape down and remove the fleshy seeds. Slice the cucumber into half moons and add to the bowl. Pull the coriander leaves from their stems and add most of them to the bowl. Drain the noodles and edamame beans and add to the bowl, *making sure not to catch any ice cubes!* Add the soy sauce, then toss together, taste and season well with salt and pepper. Add a splash of water if the salad looks at all clumpy.

3] Transfer to a platter or bowls and top with the remaining coriander leaves, the toasted sesame seeds and chilli flakes. Serve with lime wedges and Sriracha for extra heat and fun!

French

SERVES 4
TIME 30 mins
VIBE Showing off a little

NICE ON THE SIDE
Baguette, roasted chicken or fish

SALAD PARTY?
I think this is best as a fresh lunch
on its own

100g (3½oz) walnuts
2 shallots
1 teaspoon olive oil
160g (5¾oz) pancetta (or
    bacon) lardons
1 oak leaf lettuce
1 frisée lettuce
30g (1oz) mixed soft herbs
    – *I used flat leaf parsley,*
    tarragon and chives
4 very fresh eggs
salt and pepper

DRESSING

Honey & Mustard (*see* page 16)

TOPPERS

a few of the walnuts
    (*see* above)
a few of the lardons
    (*see* above)

A bistro salad is a thing of beauty – poach your egg however you fancy, but make sure that the yolk is as runny as can be; it's basically a second dressing!

SUBS **V** Swap the pancetta for a vegetarian salty cheese.
VE Swap the pancetta for plant-based bacon, omit the eggs and swap the honey in the dressing for sugar or maple syrup.

GET AHEAD Make the dressing and roast the walnuts in advance. Cook the lardons and set aside for up to 2 hours before serving.

1] Roast the walnuts (*see* page 22), then roughly chop. Whisk up the dressing in a large mixing bowl. Peel and finely chop the shallots, then add to the dressing and set aside.

2] Line a plate with kitchen paper. Heat a frying pan over a medium-high heat, add the oil and then the lardons and sizzle for 5–7 minutes until crispy. Transfer to the lined plate to drain.

3] Separate the leaves of the lettuces – *if they look at all dirty, wash in iced water and spin to dry*. Add to the large bowl *but don't toss yet!* Pull the herb leaves from the stems and roughly chop, and slice the chives, if using. Add to the bowl.

4] Bring a large pan of water to the boil, line a plate with kitchen paper. Poach your eggs to your liking (see intro) then use a slotted spoon to remove the eggs and transfer them to the lined plate.

5] Season the salad with salt and pepper and toss well. Add most of the lardons and walnuts and toss again, then divide between bowls. Top each with a poached egg and finish with the remaining walnuts and lardons. Add a crack of black pepper and serve immediately.

Triple Tomato

SERVES 4
TIME 15 mins
VIBE Easy-peasy

NICE ON THE SIDE
Pastas, focaccia or
barbecued meats

SALAD PARTY?
Serve with Courgette & White
Bean (*see page 28*) and/or Shaved
Fennel & Orzo (*see page 47*)

450g (1lb) large tomatoes
300g (10½oz) cherry tomatoes
200g (7oz) sun-dried or semi-
dried tomatoes
100g (3½oz) pecorino cheese
salt and pepper

DRESSING
Lemon & Olive Oil (*see page 16*)

TOPPERS
Croutons (*see page 23*)
handful of basil leaves

I could have filled this book with tomato salads, but I held back and
instead chose a couple that I feel really hit the spot. This one is
packed with cherry, chunky and sun-dried tomatoes. I like to serve
the pecorino in big fat wedges, but feel free to shave it over the top
if you'd prefer.

SUBS **V** Use a vegetarian hard cheese. **VE** Use vegan Parmesan-
style 'cheese' or omit.

GET AHEAD Salt the tomatoes up to an hour in advance. Make
the croutons and dressing in advance.

1] Cut the large tomatoes into wedges. Halve the cherry tomatoes.
Put both in a large mixing bowl and season generously with salt while
you make the rest of the salad. *Salting your tomatoes removes some
of their water and consequently intensifies their flavour.*

2] Make the croutons. Whisk up the dressing in a large mixing bowl.

3] Drain the salted tomatoes in a sieve and add to the dressing.
Add the sun-dried or semi-dried tomatoes to the bowl. Toss, taste
and season with extra salt if needed. Transfer to a large plate. Cut
the pecorino into triangles and tuck into the salad, then top with the
croutons and basil leaves and a crack of black pepper.

Shaved Fennel & Orzo

SERVES 4
TIME 40 mins
VIBE Easy-peasy

NICE ON THE SIDE
Grilled fish as an alternative to the sardines

SALAD PARTY?
Serve with The Ultimate Green Salad (see page 30) and/or Prawn Cocktail (see page 175)

250g (9oz) orzo, or other small
   pasta shape of your choice
90g (3¼oz) currants or raisins
1 teaspoon Dijon mustard
1 teaspoon dried oregano
75g (2¾oz) pine nuts
2 large fennel bulbs
4 tablespoons capers
30g (1oz) soft herbs – *I used
   a mixture of dill, flat leaf
   parsley and tarragon*
salt and pepper
1 or 2 × 120g (4¼oz) cans of
   sardines, to serve (optional)

DRESSING

1½ batches Lemon & Olive Oil
   (see page 16)

TOPPERS

a few of the pine nuts
   (see above)

I make a version of this as a hot spaghetti dish, but it works so *so* well as a fresh salad. I know it SEEMS like a lot of dressing, but I usually use it all!

SUBS Ⓥ Serve with feta cheese rather than canned sardines. Ⓥᴮ Omit the sardines.

GET AHEAD Make the dressing and roast the pine nuts in advance. Cook and rinse the pasta up to 2 days in advance, then toss in a little olive oil and store in an airtight container in the refrigerator. Shave the fennel and toss in the dressing up to 2 hours in advance.

1] Bring a large pan of salted water to the boil, add the orzo (or pasta of choice) and cook according to the packet instructions. Drain and rinse with cold water until completely cooled, then drain well. *This rinses away the starch so that the pasta doesn't stick together when tossed in the salad.*

2] Whisk up the dressing in a large serving bowl, then pour off about one quarter of it and set aside for adding later if needed. Add the currants or raisins, mustard and oregano and set aside. Roast the pine nuts (see page 22).

3] Shave the fennel as thinly you can – *use a mandolin if you have one, but if not, finely slice with a very sharp knife.* Add to the bowl and toss well. Add the capers, orzo and most of the roasted pine nuts. Pull the herb leaves from the stems, add to the bowl and toss well again. Taste and season with salt and pepper, adding the remaining dressing if it needs it. Top with the remaining pine nuts and serve alongside some sardines for a real Sicilian experience!

ON THIS PAGE Ham 'n' Melon (see page 53) and Frozen Pea, Mint & Cucumber (see page 29)

Fruity

'So, you want fruit in your salad but NOT a fruit salad. Here, I like to think, the fruit is the ultimate balancer, paired with salty flavours and often spicy heat. There are some people who really think that fruit should keep its nose out of savoury dishes. I'm, unsurprisingly, not one of them and I reckon these salads are the perfect way of proving them completely wrong.'

Mango, Green Bean & Peanut

SERVES 4
TIME 20 mins
VIBE Not too tricky

NICE ON THE SIDE
Grilled prawns or spicy noodles

SALAD PARTY?
Serve with Miso Noodle, Avo & Cucumber (page 40) and/or Tomatoes With Chilli Oil (page 72)

1 red chilli
300g (10½oz) green beans
200g (7oz) Tenderstem
   broccoli
2 mangoes
1 bunch (about 100g/3½oz)
   spring onions
½ small bunch (about 15g/½oz)
   coriander
½ small bunch (about 15g/½oz)
   mint
100g (3½oz) roasted, salted
   peanuts
salt and pepper

DRESSING
Miso & Lime (*see* page 19)

TOPPERS
a few of the herbs (*see* above)
a few of the peanutes
   (*see* above)
pinch of chilli flakes

Photographed on page 50

My kinda fruity salad. It's salty and savoury thanks to the dressing, chilli and the heavy measure of salted peanuts, but the mangoes give the whole thing an extra sugary punch that I cannot get enough of.

GET AHEAD Make the dressing in advance, including the red chilli. Blanch the greens up to a day before and store in an airtight container in the refrigerator.

1] Whisk up the dressing in a large mixing bowl. Finely chop the red chilli, add to the dressing and set aside.

2] Bring a large pan of salted water to the boil, add the green beans and broccoli and cook for 2–3 minutes until bright green. Drain and rinse with cold water until completely cooled, then drain well. *Alternatively, you can plunge them into a bowl of iced water and then drain*. Set aside on kitchen paper to dry.

3] Use a peeler to peel each mango, then slice off each cheek either side of the flat stone and finely slice. Add the drained greens and mango to the dressing. Finely slice the spring onions and add to the bowl. Pull the herb leaves from the stems, roughly chop and add most to the bowl. Roughly chop the peanuts and add most of them to the bowl too. Season with salt and pepper and toss well.

4] Transfer to a plate and top with the remaining herbs and peanuts, then add the chilli flakes for an extra touch of spice!

Ham 'n' Melon

SERVES 4
TIME 20 mins
VIBE Easy-peasy

NICE ON THE SIDE
Other salads for a big fresh summer lunch

SALAD PARTY?
Serve with Triple Tomato (*see* page 44) and/or Frozen Pea, Mint & Cucumber (*see* page 29)

2 shallots
olive oil
200g (7oz) prosciutto or Parma ham
1 large cantaloupe melon
2 × 150g (5½oz) balls of mozzarella cheese
pepper

DRESSING
Lemon & Olive Oil (*see* page 16)

TOPPERS
½ small bunch (about 15g/½oz) basil
½ small bunch (about 15g/½oz) mint
pinch of chilli flakes (optional)

I couldn't not. Ham and melon is the fruity salad that everyone has a little love affair with. However, once you've made this crispy ham for the top, you'll never go back to a simpler version of this classic again.

SUBS **V** Omit the ham, and make sure your mozzarella is vegetarian. **VE** Omit the ham and the mozzarella and add a handful of roasted nuts and some plant-based bacon instead.

GET AHEAD Make the dressing in advance.

1] Whisk up the dressing in a mixing bowl. Peel and finely slice the shallots into rings, then add to the dressing and set aside.

2] Heat a tiny splash of olive oil in a frying pan over a medium high-heat. Line a plate with kitchen paper. Use scissors to cut 50g (1¾oz) of the prosciutto or Parma ham into strips directly into the pan. Fry for about 5 minutes until crispy. Transfer to the lined plate to drain. *Alternatively, you can roast the ham on a baking tray lined with nonstick baking paper in the oven preheated to 200°C/180°C fan/400°F/Gas Mark 6 for 10 minutes.*

3] Halve the melon and deseed. Cut each half into about 6 wedges, then slide the knife along the base of each wedge in turn to separate the flesh from the skin. Pile on to a platter. Tear the mozzarella balls into pieces and snuggle them into the melon.

4] Tear up the remaining ham and add it to the platter. Spoon over the shallot rings and dressing – *you might not need it all here, depending on how tasty/juicy the melon is!* Top with the crispy ham. Pull the herb leaves from the stems and sprinkle over the salad, then finish with a crack of black pepper and, if using, the chilli flakes.

Pear, Pecorino & Chicory

SERVES 4
TIME 20 mins
VIBE Not too tricky

NICE ON THE SIDE
Pan-fried duck breast, simple pasta or risotto

SALAD PARTY?
Serve with Mushroom & Barley (*see page 122*) and/or Pumpkin & Burrata (*see page 184*)

75g (2¾oz) dried cherries

100g (3½oz) pitted black olives

100g (3½oz) walnuts

2 heads of chicory

100g (3½oz) watercress or rocket

125g (4½oz) pecorino, or Parmesan, cheese

½ small bunch (about 15g/½oz) flat leaf parsley

½ small bunch (about 15g/½oz) tarragon

2 pickled walnuts, chopped (optional)

2 pears

salt and pepper

DRESSING

Honey & Mustard (*see page 16*)

TOPPERS

a little of the pecorino (or Parmesan)

a few of the walnuts (*see above*)

a few of the herbs (*see above*)

Sometimes, in the winter, I have a roast dinner and kind of wish that I was eating the roasted meat and a big juicy winter salad. THIS GUY, teamed with a crackling-heavy belly of pork, is what dreams are made of.

SUBS **V** Use a vegetarian hard cheese. **VE** Swap the honey in the dressing for sugar or maple syrup and use vegan Parmesan-style 'cheese' instead.

GET AHEAD Make the dressing and roast the walnuts in advance.

1] Whisk up the dressing in a large mixing bowl. Add the dried cherries and then the olives, breaking the olives up with your hands as you go. Roast the walnuts (*see page 22*).

2] Separate the chicory leaves and add to the bowl (*don't toss!*), then add the watercress or rocket. Use a peeler to shave most of the cheese directly into the bowl. Pull the herb leaves from the stems, roughly chop and add most to the bowl, along with most of the roasted walnuts and the pickled walnuts, if using. Season generously with salt and pepper and toss together.

3] Slice the pears lengthways into quarters, then cut away the core from each quarter and cut into 5mm (¼-inch) slices. Add to the bowl and gently toss again – *you don't want to break up the pears!* Transfer to a serving platter, then shave over the remaining cheese and sprinkle over the remaining roasted walnuts and herbs.

Peach Panzanella

NICE ON THE SIDE
Barbecued meats or veggies

SALAD PARTY?
Serve with Red Pepper & Bavette (see page 159) and/or Brown Butter Greens (see page 172)

Fennel Croutons (see page 23)
4–6 peaches, depending on size (or nectarines)
olive oil
200g (7oz) watercress or rocket
1 small bunch (about 30g/1oz) flat leaf parsley
1 small bunch (about 30g/1oz) basil
2 or 3 × 125g (4½oz) balls of burrata cheese – or use mozzarella if you're feeling less fancy!
salt and pepper

DRESSING

Salsa Verde (see page 17) or Lemon & Olive Oil (see page 16)

TOPPERS

50g (1¾oz) pickled red onion (see page 23), optional
a few of the herb leaves (see above)

I used a really big burrata here, but you can definitely use 2–3 smaller balls and snuggle them down the length of the salad. You can also skip charring the peaches if you want to go for a fresher take on this!

SUBS 🅥 Make sure your burrata (or mozzarella) is vegetarian. 🆅🅔 Omit the burrata.

GET AHEAD Make the croutons and the dressing in advance. Make the pickled red onion in advance, if using.

1] Pickle the red onion, if using. Meanwhile, make the croutons, and blitz or whisk up your chosen dressing.

2] Heat a griddle pan over a high heat. Slice each peach (or nectarine) in half and remove the stone, then cut the halves into wedges. Brush with a little oil, add to the hot pan and griddle for 2–3 minutes on each side. Transfer to a large mixing bowl. Add the croutons along with the watercress or rocket. Pull the herb leaves from the stems and add most of them to the bowl. Add half of the dressing, then toss, taste and season with salt and pepper.

3] Transfer to a platter. Snuggle the burratas into the salad. Drizzle with the remaining dressing. Top with the remaining herb leaves and, if using, the pickled red onion, along with a big pinch of salt and crack of black pepper.

ON THIS PAGE: Peach Panzanella (see page 55)

Apple, Pecan & Kale

SERVES 4
TIME 20 mins
VIBE Not too tricky

NICE ON THE SIDE
Roast chicken or pork chops

SALAD PARTY?
Serve with Celeriac, Barley & Walnut (*see* pages 128–129) and/ or Cauli Wedge (*see* page 139)

100g (3½oz) pecan nuts

200g (7oz) kale or cavolo nero, stalks removed

1 head of broccoli (about 225g/8oz)

2 apples

½ small bunch (about 15g/½oz) flat leaf parsley

½ small bunch (about 15g/½oz) mint

125g (4½oz) Cheshire or Cheddar cheese

DRESSING

Honey & Mustard (*see* page 16), plus juice of 1 lemon (about 2 tablespoons)

TOPPERS

a few of the pecan nuts (*see* above)

I'm not going to lie to you – you really do need to massage the kale in the dressing here. I've been served kale all wrong so many times, and the truth is if you're not gonna cook it (preferably in a ton of olive oil, seasoned with a hefty amount of salt and finished with lemon juice), then you have to KINDA cook it, using the acidity of the dressing to break down the kale and make it edible, rather than punishing yourself with chewy mouthfuls of kale.

SUBS 🅥🅔 Use vegan Cheddar-style 'cheese' or omit, and swap the honey in the dressing for sugar or maple syrup.

GET AHEAD Roast the pecans and make the dressing in advance. Massage the kale up to an hour before – it'll just go on softening!

1] Roast the pecans (*see* page 22), then roughly chop.

2] Whisk up the dressing in a large serving bowl, then whisk in the lemon juice. Slice the kale into 1cm (½-inch) strips, add to the dressing and toss. Stand the broccoli head upside down on a chopping board. Use a knife to slice down around the head, shaving off small chunks of the broccoli florets as you go, then add to the bowl. *Save the stalk and fry it up with other veggies!* Use your hands to massage the dressing into kale and broccoli – *it takes 3–5 minutes to soften the kale to the point where it'll be great to eat.*

3] Quarter the apples, then cut away the core from each quarter and cut into 5mm (¼-inch) slices. Add to the bowl along with most of the pecans. Pull the herb leaves from the stems, roughly chop and add to the bowl. Grate the cheese and add to the bowl. Give everything a good toss, then transfer to bowls, top with the remaining pecans and serve.

Watermelon & Feta

SERVES 4
TIME 15 mins
VIBE Easy-peasy

NICE ON THE SIDE
Barbecued meats or vegetables

SALAD PARTY?
Serve with Spicy Chicken & Peanut (page 78) and/or Red Pepper & Bavette (pages 159–161)

1 red onion
1.5kg (3lb 5oz) watermelon –
    straight from the refrigerator
1 cucumber
200g (7oz) feta cheese
salt and pepper

DRESSING
Lemon & Olive Oil (*see* page 16)

TOPPERS
30g (1oz) sesame seeds
handful of mint leaves

This was a prime candidate for a salad that could teeter on the fruit salad side of things, but then I covered it in cheese and pickled red onion and everything was all right again.

SUBS 🟢 Use vegan feta-style 'cheese'.

GET AHEAD Make the dressing and toast the sesame seeds in advance.

1] Whisk up the dressing in a mixing bowl. Peel and finely slice the red onion, then add to the dressing and set aside. Toast the sesame seeds (*see* page 22).

2] Cut the watermelon in half. Place one half, flesh-side down, on a chopping board and cut into slices. Cut each slice into 4 wedges, then cut off the skin from each. Repeat with the other watermelon half. Pile the watermelon on to a platter. Cut the cucumber in half lengthways, then use a spoon to scrape down and remove the fleshy seeds. Slice the cucumber on the diagonal into half moons, then snuggle between the watermelon wedges.

3] Crumble the feta over the watermelon and cucumber, season generously with salt and pepper and then drizzle the red onion and dressing over the top. Top with the toasted sesame seeds and mint leaves and serve.

Fig & Feta

SERVES 4
TIME 35 mins
VIBE Not too tricky

NICE ON THE SIDE
Lamb, flatbreads and labneh

SALAD PARTY?
Serve with Squash & Freekeh (page 136) or Lamb Meatballs with Charred Courgettes (page 150)

12 figs

1 tablespoon clear honey

3 tablespoons olive oil

1 tablespoon pomegranate molasses

2 Gem lettuces or heads of radicchio or endive

½ small bunch (about 15g/½oz) mint

½ small bunch (about 15g/½oz) flat leaf parsley

100g (3½oz) pomegranate seeds

120g (4¼oz) pitted black olives

200g (7oz) feta cheese

salt and pepper

DRESSING

Tahini (*see page 16*)

TOPPERS

30g (1oz) sesame seeds

a few of the herbs (*see above*)

This will always be one of my faves. There's something about the sticky roasted figs with the fresh leaves and feta that works a kind of magic.

SUBS Ⓥ Swap the honey for maple syrup and use vegan feta-style 'cheese' or omit.

GET AHEAD Roast the figs up to 2 hours in advance and keep at room temperature. Toast the sesame seeds and make the dressing in advance.

1] Preheat the oven to 180°C/160°C fan/350°F/Gas Mark 4. Line a baking tray with foil. Halve the figs and place them, cut-side up, on the lined tray. Drizzle with the honey and 1 tablespoon of the oil, season with salt and pepper and roast for 20 minutes. Remove from the oven and set aside for about 10 minutes until cool enough to handle.

2] Meanwhile, toast the sesame seeds (*see page 22*). Whisk up the dressing in a bowl. Whisk the remaining oil with the pomegranate molasses in a seperate large mixing bowl and season with salt and pepper.

3] Separate the leaves of the lettuces – *if they look at all dirty, wash in iced water and spin to dry* – and add to the bowl of oil and pomegranate molasses. Pull the herb leaves from the stems and add most of them to the bowl along with the pomegranate seeds and olives. Toss the ingredients together to combine, then pile on to a platter.

4] Break the feta into rough chunks and nestle into the salad along with the roasted figs. Drizzle with the dressing. Top with the toasted sesame seeds and the remaining herb leaves.

Persimmon Caprese

SERVES 4
TIME 10 mins
VIBE Easy-peasy

NICE ON THE SIDE
Steak and chips or chicken tray bake

SALAD PARTY?
Serve with Winter Panzanella (*see* page 116) or Leeks & Cannellini Beans (*see* page 125)

2 × 250g (9oz) balls of mozzarella cheese
3–4 persimmons
140g (5oz) slices of Parma ham
salt and pepper

DRESSING
2–3 tablespoons olive oil – *use a good-quality one*
1 tablespoon balsamic vinegar

TOPPERS
handful of basil leaves

You've probably seen a persimmon in the fruit and veg section of the supermarket, only to walk on by the kind of weird peachy apple hybrid. However, walk on by no more because, through this salad, the persimmon provides us all with a way to enjoy caprese salads in that half of the year when all the tomatoes taste like water.

SUBS **V** Make sure your mozzarella is vegetarian. **VG** Use a vegan mozzarella-style 'cheese' and swap the Parma ham for sliced seasonal veggies, then layer with the persimmon in the same way.

GET AHEAD Make the dressing in advance.

1] Cut the mozzarella balls into 1cm (½-inch) slices. Slice the persimmons. Layer the mozzarella with the persimmon and Parma ham on a platter or plates, alternating between them as you go.

2] Drizzle with the oil and balsamic vinegar. Top with the basil leaves and season really well with salt and pepper.

Duck & Orange

SERVES 4
TIME 35 mins
VIBE Showing off a little

NICE ON THE SIDE
Fried rice and prawn crackers

SALAD PARTY?
Serve with Tomatoes With Chilli Oil (*see* page 72) and/or Smashed Cucumber (*see* page 75)

thumb-sized chunk of fresh root ginger

4 duck breasts

1 teaspoon five-spice powder

1 tablespoon hoisin sauce

1 large cucumber

½ bunch (about 50g/1¾oz) spring onions

1 small bunch (about 30g/1oz) coriander

2 Gem lettuces

100g (3½oz) rocket or watercress

2 oranges

salt

DRESSING
Chilli & Lime (*see* page 19)

TOPPERS
a few of the coriander leaves (*see* above)

This is the ticket for an ultimate wintery dinner, where you want to show off a bit but also not so much that you have to spend all day cooking.

SUBS **V** **VE** Swap the duck for jackfruit, tossing it in the five-spice powder and cooking it in sesame oil with soy and hoisin sauces.

GET AHEAD Make the dressing in advance. Cook and shred the duck up to 24 hours in advance, then store in an airtight container in the refrigerator. When ready to serve, just add the duck to the hot frying pan and crisp up as in step 2.

1] Whisk up the dressing in a large mixing bowl. Peel the ginger and slice into matchsticks (or grate), then add to the dressing and set aside.

2] Preheat the oven to 200°C/180°C fan/400°F/Gas Mark 6. Heat a frying pan over a medium heat. Toss the duck breasts in the five-spice and season with a pinch of salt, then add to the pan, skin-side down, and cook for 5–6 minutes until the skin is crispy. Transfer to a baking tray, brush with the hoisin sauce and roast for 10 minutes. Set aside to rest.

3] Meanwhile, cut the cucumber in half lengthways, then use a spoon to scrape down and remove the fleshy seeds. Slice the cucumber into half moons, finely slice the spring onions and add to the dressing along with most of the coriander leaves. Separate the leaves of the lettuces – *if they look at all dirty, wash in iced water and spin to dry* – add to the bowl, along with the rocket and watercress and toss it all together. Tip onto a platter. Slice the duck into 1cm (½ inch) slices and add to the salad.

4] Peel the oranges, removing as much white pith as possible. Slice into rounds or segments. Snuggle the orange pieces into the salad. Finish with a pinch of salt, and top with the remaining coriander leaves.

Strawberry, Mint & Hazelnut

SERVES 4
TIME 10 mins
VIBE Easy-peasy

NICE ON THE SIDE
Barbecued chicken, pork chops or steak

SALAD PARTY?
Serve with Triple Tomato (*see* page 44) and/or Lamb Meatballs with Charred Courgettes (*see* page 150)

100g (3½oz) blanched hazelnuts
500g (1lb 2oz) strawberries
1 small bunch (about 30g/1oz) mint
1 small bunch (about 30g/1oz) basil
200g (7oz) lamb's lettuce or watercress
160g (5¾oz) pitted black olives
100g (3½oz) ricotta salata (salted ricotta), or pecorino or Parmesan cheese
salt and pepper

DRESSING

Lemon & Olive Oil (*see* page 16)

TOPPERS

a few of the hazelnuts (*see* above)

This is the perfect summer salad. There, I said it. Why? Well, it takes 10 minutes to make, and it's cool, refreshing, salty and light enough to eat in the blinding sun.

SUBS Ⓥ Use a vegetarian hard cheese. Ⓥᴱ Use vegan Parmesan-style 'cheese' or omit.

GET AHEAD Roast the hazelnuts and make the dressing in advance.

1] Roast the hazelnuts (*see* page 22).

2] Whisk up the dressing in a large mixing bowl. Hull the strawberries, then halve and add to the dressing. Pull the herb leaves from the stems and add to the bowl along with the lamb's lettuce or watercress. Then add the olives, crushing them with your hands to break them up as you go. Use a peeler to shave the cheese directly into the bowl. Roughly crush or halve the hazelnuts and add most of them to the bowl.

3] Season well with salt and pepper, then toss everything well. Transfer to bowls or a platter, top with the remaining hazelnuts and finish with a crack of black pepper.

Hot 'n' Spicy

'Every now and then, I get in and all I want to do is eat an entire jar of chilli oil over vegetables. Luckily, I've managed to channel that craving into some far more delicious recipes that balance out the spice levels. If you're not a hot sauce fanatic or chilli oil enthusiast, adjust the spicy elements accordingly. And if you are... I like to serve (myself) with extra on the side, to continue loading as I go.'

Tomatoes with Chilli Oil

SERVES 4
TIME 35 mins
VIBE Easy-peasy

NICE ON THE SIDE
Spatchcocked chicken or spicy noodles

SALAD PARTY?
Serve with Spicy Chicken & Peanut (*see* page 78) and/or Bombay Potato (*see* page 94)

1kg (2lb 4oz) mixed large and cherry tomatoes

1 cucumber

½ bunch (about 50g/1¾oz) spring onions

½ small bunch (about 15g/½oz) Thai basil

½ small bunch (about 15g/½oz) mint

1 tablespoon fish sauce

1 lime

salt and pepper

DRESSING

Chilli & Lime (*see* page 19), swapping the chilli sauce for 2 tablespoons chilli oil (such as Lee Kum Kee, or *see* page 25 for homemade)

TOPPERS

30g (1oz) sesame seeds

a few of the herb leaves (*see* above)

Tomato salad number 2. I feel like the picture does the talking here; I don't need to convince you that those pools of chilli oil dressing are heaven-sent. I will, however, URGE you to buy the best tomatoes you can find. A tomato salad is only as good as its tomatoes, and if you get the good 'uns here, you'll be treated to the best tomato salad you could ever dream of. And if you use a shop-bought chilli oil, try to get one with the most chilli bits in it, not just chilli flavoured.

SUBS **V** **VE** Omit the fish sauce.

GET AHEAD Make the dressing in advance. Slice and salt the tomatoes and cucumbers up to an hour in advance.

1] Chop the large tomatoes into wedges. Halve the cherry tomatoes. Cut the cucumber into 2cm (¾-inch) chunks. Put in a large bowl with the tomatoes along with a big pinch of salt and set aside for about 30 minutes (*if you're in a rush, just leave while you make the dressing*).

2] Meanwhile, make the chilli oil, if using homemade. Toast the sesame seeds (*see* page 22). Whisk up the dressing.

3] Drain the tomatoes and cucumber and return them to the bowl. Slice the spring onions and add to the bowl. Pull the herb leaves from the stems and add most of them to the bowl along with the fish sauce. Season with salt and pepper. Transfer to a plate. Drizzle with the dressing – *you might not need it all* – and top with the remaining herb leaves and toasted sesame seeds. Cut the lime into wedges and serve on the side. Serve with extra chilli oil, if you like.

Smashed Cucumber

SERVES 4
TIME 30 mins
VIBE Easy-peasy

NICE ON THE SIDE
Pan-fried chicken or duck breast,
fried Asian greens or
roasted aubergine

SALAD PARTY?
Serve with Poached Ginger
Chicken (page 32) and/or
Tomatoes With Chilli Oil (page 72)

200g (7oz) radishes

2 large cucumbers

300g (10½oz) jasmine or
    basmati rice

600ml (20fl oz) water

1 bunch (about 100g/3½oz)
    spring onions

1 small bunch (about 30g/1oz)
    coriander

1 small bunch (about 30g/1oz)
    mint

4 tablespoons tahini

4 tablespoons chilli oil (such as
    Lee Kum Kee, or *see* page 25
    for homemade)

salt

DRESSING
Miso & Lime (*see* page 19), plus
    1 tablespoon soy sauce

TOPPERS
a few of the herbs (*see* above)

When you team cold, juicy, salted cucumbers with tahini and chilli oil, you get a genuine flavour bomb that I'd love to take credit for, but the combo has been around long before me.

GET AHEAD Make the dressing and, if using, toast the sesame seeds in advance. Cook and rinse the rice up to 2 days in advance, then store in an airtight container in the refrigerator.

1] Whisk up the dressing including the soy in a mixing bowl. Finely slice the radishes, add to the dressing and set aside.

2] Use a rolling pin to bash each cucumber until it splits open. Roughly cut the cucumbers into chunks, add to a large bowl with a big pinch of salt and set aside in the refrigerator while you prepare the rest of the salad.

3] Rinse the rice in a sieve until the water runs clear. Put into a saucepan, pour in the measured water and add a big pinch of salt. Bring to the boil, then cover with a lid, reduce the heat to a very gentle simmer and cook for 10 minutes. Remove from the heat and set aside with the lid on for 5 minutes.

4] Meanwhile, slice the spring onions and put in a large mixing bowl. Pull the herb leaves from the stems. Finely slice the coriander stems and add to the bowl, then roughly chop the mint and coriander leaves together and add most to the bowl.

5] Rinse the rice with cold water until completely cooled, then drain well. Add half of the dressing and half of the radishes to the bowl, then the cooled rice and toss well. Taste and season with salt and pepper, then spoon into bowls or on to a platter.

6] Drain the cucumber in a sieve and add to the empty bowl along with the remaining dressing and radishes. Toss, then pile on top of the rice. Drizzle the tahini and chilli oil over the salad, then top with remaining herbs.

Spicy Steak

SERVES 4
TIME 40 mins
VIBE Not too tricky

NICE ON THE SIDE
Big green salad and flatbreads

SALAD PARTY?
Serve with Potato Salad: The Boiled One (*see* page 181) and/or Chop Chop Feta (*see* page 185)

400g (14oz) tomatoes
1 small red onion
juice of 1 lemon (about 2 tablespoons)
Crispy Chickpeas (*see* page 24)
2–3 sirloin steaks (about 500g/1lb 2oz in total)
3 tablespoons olive oil
2 garlic cloves
1½ teaspoons hot paprika
1 small bunch (about 30g/1oz) flat leaf parsley or coriander
salt and pepper

DRESSING
Tahini (*see* page 16), plus 1 tablespoon harissa

TOPPERS
a few of the crispy chickpeas (*see* above)
a few of the herb leaves (*see* above)

Harissa is the kitchen secret that'll serve you well every time.

SUBS Ⓥ Ⓥ🄴 Swap the steaks for 4 charred aubergine halves.

GET AHEAD Make the crispy chickpeas and dressing in advance.

1] Roughly chop the tomatoes into 3cm (1¼-inch) chunks. Put in a bowl, season generously with salt and set aside. *This removes the water from the tomatoes and makes them taste 10 times better!* Peel and finely slice the red onion, add to another bowl. Cover with the lemon juice, add a big pinch of salt and a splash of boiling water and set aside to pickle. Make the crispy chickpeas.

2] Meanwhile, make the dressing, adding the harissa – this will thicken the dressing, but keep whisking and slowly trickling in extra water until it reaches a drizzling consistency.

3] Heat a large nonstick frying pan over a high heat. Rub the steaks with 1 tablespoon of the olive oil and season well, then add to the hot pan and fry for 1½ minutes on each side (for medium). Set aside. Turn the heat off under the pan.

4] Add the remaining 2 tablespoons oil to the pan. Peel and finely slice the garlic, then add to the pan with the smoked paprika – the pan will still be hot enough to lightly colour them both, but scrape it a bit to pick up some of the meaty goodness! Transfer the garlic, paprika and any oil in the pan to a large mixing bowl.

5] Add most of the crispy chickpeas to the bowl, then drain the tomatoes and add those along with the pickled onions and most of the herb leaves. Season well and toss. Transfer to a platter or plates.

6] Slice the steaks, then snuggle the slices into the salad. Drizzle the dressing and top with the remaining crispy chickpeas and herb leaves.

Spicy Chicken & Peanut

SERVES 4
TIME 40 mins, plus cooking
VIBE Easy-peasy

NICE ON THE SIDE
Egg fried rice or spicy noodles

SALAD PARTY?
Serve with Tomatoes With Chilli Oil (*see page 72*) and/or Thai Red Aubergine (*see page 86*)

6 boneless, skinless chicken thighs

2 tablespoons olive oil

1 large cucumber

3 Gem lettuces

6 spring onions

100g (3½oz) roasted, salted peanuts

1 small bunch (about 30g/1oz) coriander

1 small bunch (about 30g/1oz) mint

salt and pepper

DRESSING

Chilli & Lime (*see page 19*), plus 2 tablespoons peanut butter

TOPPERS

pinch of chilli flakes

3–4 tablespoons crispy onions

It's half a love of peanut butter and half a love of a crowd-pleaser that made me develop this salad. Serve it up as the perfect fail-safe for impressing, and feel free to up the peanut butter if you too have a penchant for a little too much.

SUBS **V** **VE** Swap the chicken thighs for pan-fried strips of firm tofu.

GET AHEAD Make the dressing in advance. Roast and shred the chicken thighs up to 2 days in advance, then store in an airtight container in the refrigerator.

1] Preheat the oven to 200°C/180°C fan/400°F/Gas Mark 6. Lay the chicken thighs on a baking tray, drizzle with the oil and roast for 15–20 minutes until cooked through. Remove from the oven and use 2 forks to shred into strips, then set aside to cool a little.

2] Meanwhile, whisk up the dressing including the peanut butter until well combined.

3] Cut the cucumber in half lengthways, then slice into half moons and put in a large mixing bowl. Separate the leaves of the lettuces – *if they look at all dirty, wash in iced water and spin to dry* – and finely slice the spring onions, then add both to the bowl. Roughly chop most of the peanuts and add to the bowl. Pull the herb leaves from the stems and roughly chop, then add to the bowl. Add the dressing and toss to combine.

4] Add the chicken to the salad and toss again, then taste and season well with salt and pepper. Transfer to a large platter and top with the chilli flakes and crispy onions.

Spicy Noodle

SERVES 4
TIME 20 mins
VIBE Not too tricky

NICE ON THE SIDE
Soy-glazed chicken thighs or sticky pork ribs

SALAD PARTY?
Serve with Duck & Orange (*see* page 66) and/or Spicy Chicken & Peanut (*see* page 78)

200g (7oz) rice noodles
1 teaspoon Sichuan peppercorns (optional)
1 teaspoon chilli flakes
1 red chilli
½ red cabbage (about 350g/12oz)
220g (7¾oz) frozen peas
½ bunch (about 50g/1¾oz) spring onions
1 small bunch (about 30g/1oz) coriander
100g (3½oz) roasted, salted peanuts
1 lime
chilli oil, to serve (such as Lee Kum Kee, or *see* page 25 for homemade), optional
soy sauce, to serve (optional)

DRESSING
Chilli & Lime (*see* page 19), swapping 2 tablespoons of the oil for 2 tablespoons peanut butter and adding 2 tablespoons water

TOPPERS
a few of the peanuts (*see* above)
a few of the coriander leaves (*see* above)

This is inspired by a recipe from Meera Sodha that I've cooked loads. She makes her own chilli oil and drizzles it all over the shop – it's incredible! I've made this salad with Sichuan peppercorns, peas and peanuts because what can possibly go wrong with those ingredients.

GET AHEAD Cook and rinse the rice noodles up to 24 hours in advance, then toss in a little oil and store in an airtight container in the refrigerator. Make the dressing in advance. Toss the red cabbage in the dressing up to 2 hours in advance.

1] Put the rice noodles into a large bowl, cover with boiling water and set aside until softened – *keep checking, as depending on the brand this can take anywhere between 4 and 10 minutes*. Drain and rinse with cold water until completely cooled, then drain well.

2] Whisk up the dressing in a large mixing bowl, adding the peanut butter and measured water. Heat a dry frying pan over a medium heat, add the peppercorns, if using, and toast for about 2 minutes until fragrant. Blitz them in a spice grinder or crush with a pestle and mortar, then add to the dressing along with the chilli flakes. Finely chop the red chilli and add to the dressing.

3] Slice the red cabbage as finely as you can – *use a mandolin if you have one* – then add to the bowl and toss. Add the frozen peas – *they'll defrost as you finish* – and then toss the salad. Slice the spring onions and add to the bowl. Pull the coriander leaves from the stems, then finely slice the stems and add to the bowl along with most of the leaves.

4] Chop or crush the peanuts and toss most of them into the bowl. Add the rice noodles, then toss, taste and add extra chilli oil or soy as needed. Transfer to bowls or a platter. Top with the remaining peanuts and coriander leaves. I like to serve this with more chilli oil for an extra kick!

Thai Larb

SERVES 4
TIME 25 mins
VIBE Not too tricky

NICE ON THE SIDE
Papaya salad and sticky rice

SALAD PARTY?
Thai Red Aubergine (*see* page 86) and/or Grilled Nutty Greens (*see* page 143)

2 banana shallots
2 garlic cloves
thumb-sized chunk of fresh root ginger
1 lemon grass stalk
1 red chilli
1 tablespoon vegetable or sunflower oil
500g (1lb 2oz) minced pork – *get the fattiest you can find!*
½ bunch (50g/1¾oz) spring onions
1 cucumber
3 Gem lettuces
½ small bunch (about 15g/½oz) coriander
½ small bunch (about 15g/½oz) mint
½ small bunch (about 15g/½oz) Thai basil (optional)
1 lime
salt and pepper

DRESSING

Chilli & Lime (*see* page 19), plus 2 tablespoons fish sauce

TOPPERS

4 tablespoons Thai sticky rice (or jasmine rice), optional
a few of the herb leaves (*see* above)

I really urge you to give the toasted rice a go, as it not only adds a nutty flavour but provides a crunch that makes the salad even more moreish. Make sure you cook the rice until dark golden, tossing the pan regularly, so that you don't end up with a raw rice situation on your hands!

SUBS Ⓥ ⓋⒼ Swap the minced pork for minced tofu and omit the fish sauce.

GET AHEAD Toast and blitz the rice up to a week in advance, then store in an airtight container, if using. Make the dressing in advance.

1] If making the toasted rice topper, put the rice in a dry frying pan and toast over a medium-low heat for 15–20 minutes until it turns a dark golden colour and smells like popcorn. Put into a blender and blitz to a coarse powder. Transfer to a bowl and set aside. Whisk up the dressing in a large mixing bowl along with the fish sauce.

2] Peel the shallots, garlic and ginger, and roughly slice the lemon grass and red chilli. Add all to the blender or a mini chopper and blitz to a coarse paste. Set aside.

3] Heat the oil in a large frying pan over a medium-high heat, add the minced pork and use a spatula to break it up a little. Fry for 15 minutes until cooked through and golden in places. Add the paste and fry for 5–7 minutes, then remove the pan from the heat. Add a big splash of the dressing along with a generous pinch of salt. Stir well and set aside.

4] Slice the spring onions and dice the cucumber into about 1cm (½-inch) cubes, then add both to the bowl of dressing. Separate the leaves of the lettuces and add them to the bowl. Pull the herb leaves from the stems and add most of them to the bowl. Toss, taste and season with salt and pepper. Transfer to plates with the crispy pork mixture and top with the toasted rice, if using, and remaining herb leaves. Cut the lime into wedges and serve on the side.

Vermicelli Chicken

SERVES 4
TIME 40 mins
VIBE Showing off a little

NICE ON THE SIDE
Perfect simply with a cold beer – and maybe some spring rolls!

SALAD PARTY?
Serve with Tomatoes With Chilli Oil (see page 72) and/or Grilled Nutty Greens (see page 143)

1 chubby garlic clove

2 tablespoons fish sauce

6 boneless, skinless chicken thighs

150g (5oz) vermicelli noodles (4 nests)

200g (7oz) bean sprouts

2 large carrots, peeled

1 large cucumber

1 red chilli

½ small bunch (about 15g/½oz) coriander

½ small bunch (about 15g/½oz) mint

salt

lime wedges, to serve

DRESSING

2 batches Chilli & Lime (see page 19), swapping the chilli sauce for sweet chilli sauce

TOPPERS

3–4 tablespoons crispy onions or 50g (1¾oz) roasted, salted peanuts

Inspired by my favourite order whenever I get a Vietnamese takeaway, I tried to get this as close to the real deal as I could. Using chicken thighs is key so that their juiciness adds a kind of second dressing to the noodles.

SUBS Ⓥ ⓋⒻ Swap the chicken for 2 aubergines, halved, drizzled with a few tablespoons of the dressing and roasted, and omit the fish sauce.

GET AHEAD Make the dressing in advance. Marinate the chicken up to 24 hours in advance in an airtight container in the refrigerator.

1] Whisk up the dressing in a large mixing bowl. Finely grate or crush the garlic into the dressing, add the fish sauce and set aside. Rub the chicken thighs with 2–3 tablespoons of the dressing. Cover and leave to marinate in the refrigerator while you prepare the noodles.

2] Put the noodles into a large bowl and cover with boiling water. Use a fork to gently tease them out of their nests, then set aside for about 5 minutes until softened. Drain and rinse with cold water until completely cooled. Tip into the large mixing bowl of remaining dressing.

3] Heat a large frying pan over a high heat, and once hot, add the chicken thighs and fry for 3–4 minutes on each side, or until cooked through. Set aside on a chopping board and season with a little salt.

4] Add the bean sprouts to the noodles. Use a peeler to peel the carrots and cucumber into ribbons directly into the bowl of noodles – *discard the seedy middle of the cucumber*. Finely chop the red chilli and add to the bowl along with the leaves from the herbs. Toss really well.

5] Pile into bowls or a platter. Slice the chicken thighs and add on top. Sprinkle with the remaining herb leaves and crispy onions or peanuts. Serve with lime wedges.

Thai Red Aubergine

SERVES 4
TIME 40 mins
VIBE Showing off a little

NICE ON THE SIDE
Barbecued chicken or
Thai-style greens

SALAD PARTY?
Serve with Tomatoes With Chilli
Oil (see page 72) and/or
Thai Larb (see page 82)

3 aubergines
2–3 tablespoons Thai red
　curry paste
4 tablespoons sesame oil
250g (9oz) jasmine or basmati
　rice
500ml (18fl oz) water
1 lime
1 cucumber
1 bunch (about 100g/3½oz)
　spring onions
1 red chilli
½ small bunch (about 15g/½oz)
　coriander
½ small bunch (about 15g/½oz)
　mint
100g (3½oz) roasted, salted
　peanuts
salt and pepper

DRESSING

150g (5½oz) natural yogurt
2 tablespoons peanut butter
juice of 1 lime (about
　1 tablespoon)

TOPPERS

a few of the herbs (see above)
a few of the peanuts
　(see above)

I love to eat this whenever I make a soy-marinated barbecued chicken. It also goes GREAT with a nice green salad tossed in my Chilli & Lime dressing (see page 19).

SUBS Ⓥ Use vegan yogurt or coconut cream in the dressing.

GET AHEAD Make the dressing up to 2 days in advance, then store in an airtight jar in the refrigerator. Cook and rinse the rice up to 2 days in advance, then store in an airtight container in the refrigerator.

1] Preheat the grill to high and line a baking tray with foil. Cut the aubergines into 8 chunky wedges, put on the tray and grill for about 20 minutes until charred. Whisk together the curry paste and 2 tablespoons of the sesame oil. Once the aubergine is charred, turn the grill off and preheat the oven to 200°C/180°C fan/400°F/Gas Mark 6. Drizzle the aubergines with the curried oil and toss, then cover the tray with foil and roast for 10 minutes or until totally soft.

2] While the aubergine is cooking, rinse the rice in a sieve until the water runs clear. Put in a saucepan, pour in the measured water and add a big pinch of salt. Bring to the boil, then cover with a lid, reduce the heat to a simmer and cook for 10 minutes. Remove from the heat and after 5 minutes rinse with cold water until completely cooled. Drain well.

3] Whisk the ingredients for the dressing together, season well and add a splash of water so that it's a drizzling consistency.

4] Put the remaining sesame oil along with the zest and juice of the lime into a large mixing bowl, then whisk together. Cut the cucumber into half moons, finely slice the spring onions and red chilli and add to the bowl along with the rice. Pull the herb leaves from the stems and roughly chop along with the peanuts, add most of this to the bowl. Toss, then taste and season. Transfer to a platter, snuggle in the charred aubergines and drizzle with the dressing, then top with the remaining herbs and peanuts.

Spicy Pasta

SERVES 4
TIME 50 mins, plus cooling
VIBE Not too tricky

NICE ON THE SIDE
Green salad or steak

SALAD PARTY?
Serve with The Ultimate Green Salad (page 30) and/or Spicy Steak (page 76)

1 garlic clove

2 red chillies

2 tablespoons olive oil

2 teaspoons hot smoked paprika

1 tablespoon clear honey

460g jar of roasted red peppers

juice of 1 lemon (about 2 tablespoons)

350g (12oz) pasta shapes

1 small bunch (about 30g/1oz) flat leaf parsley

100g (3½oz) feta cheese

salt and pepper

DRESSING
Lemon & Olive Oil (see page 16)

TOPPERS
50g (1¾oz) smoked almonds

Use any small pasta shape you like here. The smoked almonds make a great finishing touch, adding a smoky crunch that people go crazy for. Omit the second chilli if you're not big on spice.

SUBS Ⓥ Use vegan feta-style 'cheese' or omit and swap the honey for brown sugar.

GET AHEAD Make the dressing in advance. Cook and rinse the pasta up to 2 days in advance, then toss in a little olive oil and store in an airtight container in the refrigerator.

1] Peel and finely slice the garlic and finely slice one of the chillies. Heat the oil in a large frying pan over a medium-high heat. Then add the garlic, chilli and smoked paprika to the pan. Add a big pinch of salt, cook for 1 minute, then remove from the heat and add the honey. Slice the roasted red peppers into strips and add to the pan along with the lemon juice, season well and set aside to cool.

2] Meanwhile, whisk up the dressing in a large mixing bowl. Core and deseed the other chilli, finely chop and add to the bowl.

3] Bring a large pan of salted water to the boil, add the pasta and cook according to the packet instructions. Drain and rinse with cold water until completely cooled, then drain well and add to the bowl.

4] Add the red pepper mixture to the bowl. Pull the parsley leaves from the stems and roughly chop, then add most to the bowl. Season generously with salt and pepper and toss well. Add the feta, breaking it into chunks with your hands, then gently toss again – *you don't want to break the feta up too much!*

5] Spoon into bowls or on to a platter and finish with the remaining parsley. Roughly chop the smoked almonds and sprinkle on top.

Baby Corn, Feta & Black Bean

SERVES 4
TIME 20 mins
VIBE Easy-peasy

NICE ON THE SIDE
Pan-fried steak or tacos

SALAD PARTY?
Serve with Courgette & White Bean (*see page 28*) and/or Red Pepper & Bavette (*see page 159*)

1 red onion
1 jalapeño
1 teaspoon clear honey
2 × 175g (6oz) packets of baby corn
vegetable or sunflower oil
2 × 400g (14oz) cans of black beans
300g (10½oz) cherry tomatoes
1 small bunch (about 30g/1oz) coriander
200g (7oz) block feta cheese
salt and pepper

DRESSING
Lemon & Olive Oil (*see page 16*), swapping the lemon juice for lime juice

TOPPERS
a little of the coriander (*see above*)
large handful of tortilla chips

My pal Anna didn't like baby corn, and went so far as to disregard this salad on account of them. HOWEVER, once they got charred and tossed with some spicy beans and cheese, she had a miraculous change of heart. If that story isn't enough to compel you to cook this, I can tell you that the spicy jalapeño dressing is the kind that you might just want to dress all your salads with, forever.

SUBS 🟢 Swap the honey for sugar and the feta for vegan feta-style 'cheese' or marinated firm tofu.

GET AHEAD Make the dressing in advance.

1] Preheat the grill to high. Meanwhile, whisk up the dressing in a large mixing bowl. Peel and finely slice the red onion and finely slice the jalapeño, then add both to the bowl with the honey. Season generously with salt and pepper, toss to combine and set aside.

2] Spread the baby corn out on a baking tray, drizzle with oil and season with salt and pepper, then grill for about 10 minutes or so until charred.

3] Meanwhile, drain and rinse the black beans, then drain well and add to the mixing bowl. Halve the cherry tomatoes and add them to the bowl. Pull the leaves from the coriander and roughly chop, then add most to the bowl and toss well.

4] Add the charred corn and toss again, then taste and season well with salt and pepper. Transfer to a platter. Break the feta into chunks and nestle into the salad. Sprinkle with the remaining coriander and break over the tortilla chips.

Spiced but Not Spicy

'My spice drawer is one of my greatest achievements. I can truly recommend buying yourself a label maker and going wild for the sake of the moment of pure joy that comes every time you open that drawer and check it out. These salads make the most of those preciously labelled jars, they're not hot lip burners, but rather dishes for when you're craving those spicy flavours without all the heat.'

Bombay Potato

SERVES 4
TIME 45 mins
VIBE Easy-peasy

NICE ON THE SIDE
Tandoori chicken, naan bread or spiced veggies

SALAD PARTY?
Serve with Spiced Chicken with Minty Yogurt (*see page 108*)

1kg (2lb 4oz) baby potatoes (or larger potatoes, halved)

1 teaspoon ground turmeric

2 tablespoons vegetable or sunflower oil

4 spring onions

½ small bunch (about 15g/½oz) coriander

½ small bunch (about 15g/½oz) mint

4 tablespoons natural yogurt

1 lime

salt and pepper

DRESSING

3 tablespoons vegetable or sunflower oil

2 chubby garlic cloves

thumb-sized chunk of fresh root ginger

1 red chilli

2 tablespoons curry powder

6–8 curry leaves (optional)

TOPPERS

2–3 tablespoons mango chutney

50g (1¾oz) Bombay mix

pinch of chilli flakes

a few of the herb leaves (*see above*)

a little of the spring onion (*see above*)

Photographed on page 92

There are three very different potato salads in this book. This one, drenched in yogurt and scattered with Bombay mix, is one of the best I've ever tested. I reckon you'll feel the same.

SUBS Ⓥ Use vegan yogurt.

GET AHEAD Boil the potatoes up to 3 days in advance, then smash and roast when you're ready to serve. Make the lime yogurt up to 2 days in advance and store in an airtight jar in the refrigerator.

1] Scrub the potatoes if dirty, then put into a large saucepan, cover with water and add the turmeric along with a big pinch of salt. Place over a high heat, bring to the boil and cook for 15–20 minutes, depending on size, or until a knife slides through them without any resistance.

2] Meanwhile, preheat the oven to 240°C/220°C fan/475°F/Gas Mark 9. To make the dressing, place a frying pan over a medium-high heat and add the oil. Peel and grate the garlic and ginger into the pan, then slice the red chilli and add to the pan along with the curry powder and curry leaves, if using, and fry for 2 minutes. Transfer to a large mixing bowl.

3] Once they're cooked, drain the potatoes, then add them to a baking tray and use a spatula to crush them a little. Drizzle with the oil and season with salt and pepper. Roast for 20–30 minutes, stirring with the spatula every 5 minutes, until crispy. Meanwhile, put the yogurt in a bowl, finely grate in the zest of the lime and squeeze in the juice, then mix together and season well.

4] Add the potatoes to the dressing and toss well. Finely slice the spring onions and add most to the bowl along with most of the herb leaves. Toss well, taste and season. Transfer to a platter.

5] Top the potatoes with the lime yogurt, mango chutney, Bombay mix and chilli flakes, finish with the remaining herb leaves and spring onions.

Za'atar Fattoush

SERVES 4
TIME 25 mins
VIBE Easy-peasy

NICE ON THE SIDE
Hummus

SALAD PARTY?
Serve with Spicy Steak (*see* page 76) and/or Cauli Wedge (*see* page 139)

1 large cucumber

6 tomatoes

1 teaspoon sumac

pinch of sugar

1 Romaine lettuce

1 small bunch (about 30g/1oz) flat leaf parsley

1 small bunch (about 30g/1oz) mint

salt and pepper

DRESSING
Lemon & Olive Oil (*see* page 16), plus 1 tablespoon pomegranate molasses

TOPPERS
Pitta Chips, using za'atar (*see* page 25)

Fattoush is up there with my all-time favourite salads. Get the freshest toms you can to really make this salad the dreamboat it's meant to be!

GET AHEAD Make the pitta chips and dressing in advance.

1] Roughly chop the cucumber and tomatoes into 3cm (1¼-inch) chunks. Put in a large bowl with a big pinch of salt and set aside.

2] Make the pitta chips. Whisk up the dressing including the pomegranate molasses.

3] Strain the cucumber and tomatoes through a large sieve set over a saucepan to catch the liquid, then return the veg to the bowl. Warm the liquid over a low heat until steaming, then add the sumac and sugar. Set aside for 5 minutes.

4] Shred the lettuce – *if it looks at all dirty, wash in iced water and spin to dry* – and add to the bowl. Pull the herb leaves from the stems and add to the bowl. Add the sumac-y water to the dressing and whisk – *or shake in a jam jar* – until it emulsifies into the dressing. Tip the dressing over the salad, season with salt and pepper and toss.

5] Just before serving, add the pitta chips and toss, then transfer to a platter.

Saffron Rice

SERVES 4
TIME 30 mins
VIBE Not too tricky

NICE ON THE SIDE
Grilled prawns or roasted
feta cheese

SALAD PARTY?
Serve with Raw Broccoli &
Almond (page 33) and/or Spiced
Aubergine & Lentil (page 111)

600g (1lb 5oz) cherry tomatoes
1 tablespoon olive oil
1 teaspoon smoked paprika
300g (10½oz) jasmine or
   basmati rice
600ml (20fl oz) water
big pinch of saffron threads
30g (1oz) mixed flat leaf parsley
   and coriander
50g (1¾oz) rocket or
   watercress
salt and pepper

DRESSING
½ batch Lemon & Olive Oil
   (see page 16)

TOPPERS
50g (1¾oz) almonds
80g (2¾oz) natural yogurt
pinch of chilli flakes
a few of the herb leaves
   (see above)

This was the result of a happy kitchen accident with leftovers of saffron rice made the previous day. The blistered tomatoes are the real star of the show, adding an extra kick to the spiced rice. Eat this hot or cold – it's delicious either way.

SUBS 🅥🅕 Use vegan yogurt for topping.

GET AHEAD Roast the tomatoes and cook and rinse the rice until completely cooled up to 2 days in advance, store in an airtight container in the refrigerator and assemble the salad to enjoy cold.

1] Preheat the grill to high. Put the tomatoes into a large roasting tray, drizzle over the oil and sprinkle with the smoked paprika, then season generously with salt and toss to coat. Grill for 15 minutes until the tomatoes are charred and bursting. Remove from the grill and set aside to cool a little. Roast the almonds (see page 22).

2] Meanwhile, rinse the rice in a sieve until the water runs clear. Put into a saucepan, pour in the measured water and add the saffron along with a big pinch of salt. Bring to the boil, then cover with a lid, reduce the heat to a very gentle simmer and cook for 10 minutes. Remove from the heat and set aside with the lid on for 5 minutes.

3] Make the dressing. Pull the herb leaves from the stems and roughly chop, then add most to the rice. Stir through half of the tomatoes.

5] Add the rocket or watercress and half of the dressing, then taste and add more of the dressing if it needs it. *You might not need as much dressing here, as the tomatoes are so juicy when roasted.* Season well with salt and pepper, then transfer to bowls or a platter. Top with the yogurt, roasted almonds, chilli flakes and remaining herb leaves and tomatoes.

Beetroot & Chickpea

SERVES 4
TIME 35 mins
VIBE Not too tricky

NICE ON THE SIDE
Pitta breads or slow-cooked lamb shoulder

SALAD PARTY?
Serve with Winter Panzanella (*see page 116*) and/or Squash & Freekeh (*see page 134*)

2 tablespoons olive oil

1 tablespoon cumin seeds

1 tablespoon ground coriander

2 × 250g (9oz) packets ready-cooked beetroot – *not in vinegar!* – or 6 beets cooked from raw (*see page 116 for instructions*)

2 × 400g (14oz) cans of chickpeas

200g (7oz) block feta cheese

200g (7oz) thick Greek yogurt

juice of ½ lemon (about 1 tablespoon)

½ small bunch (about 15g/½oz) flat leaf parsley

½ small bunch (about 15g/½oz) mint

salt and pepper

DRESSING

½ batch Lemon & Olive Oil (*see page 16*)

TOPPERS

50g (¾oz) Savoury Granola (*see page 24*), Spiced Nuts (*see page 22*), or roasted nuts

a few of the herb leaves (*see above*)

Originally from my newsletter, this had such a good reception that it had to make it into this book.

SUBS 🆅🅴 Use vegan feta-style 'cheese' and coconut yogurt or other vegan alternative, and omit the savoury granola.

GET AHEAD Make the savoury granola or spiced nuts, or roast the nuts, and make the dressing in advance. Make the feta yogurt up to 2 days in advance and store in an airtight container in the refrigerator.

1] Make the savoury granola or spiced nuts, or roast the nuts (*see page 22*).

2] Preheat the oven to 200°C/180°C fan/400°F/Gas Mark 6. Put the oil and spices in a large roasting tray and whisk to combine. Cut the beetroot into wedges and add to the tray. Drain and rinse the chickpeas, then drain well, add to the tray and season well with salt and pepper. Toss everything together, then roast for 15 minutes until the chickpeas are crispy.

3] Meanwhile, blitz the feta in a blender with 3 tablespoons of the yogurt and the lemon juice. Transfer to a bowl, then stir in the remaining yogurt. Season well.

4] Whisk up the dressing in a large mixing bowl. Pull the herb leaves from the stems and add most of them to the bowl.

5] When the chickpeas and beetroot are cooked, add to the dressing and toss.

6] Spread the feta yogurt on to a platter and top with the chickpeas and beetroot. Sprinkle with the remaining herb leaves and the savoury granola, spiced nuts or roasted nuts.

Curried Carrot & Parsnip Udon

SERVES 4
TIME 30 mins
VIBE Easy-peasy

NICE ON THE SIDE
Glazed chicken thighs or pan-fried fish

SALAD PARTY?
Serve with Sweet Potato & Miso
(*see page 135*)

100g (3½oz) cashew nuts

1 tablespoon olive oil

1 garlic clove

thumb-sized chunk of fresh root ginger

1 tablespoon cumin seeds

1 tablespoon curry powder

1 teaspoon ground coriander

1kg (2lb 4oz) mixed carrots and parsnips

600g (1lb 5oz) ready-cooked udon noodles

½ bunch (about 50g/1¾oz) spring onions

½ small bunch (about 15g/½oz) coriander

½ small bunch (about 15g/½oz) mint

1 lime

salt and pepper

DRESSING

Lemon & Olive Oil (*see page 16*), swapping the lemon juice for lime juice – *and feel free to swap 2 tablespoons of the olive oil for sesame oil*

TOPPERS

a few of the cashew nuts (*see above*)

a few of the herbs (*see above*)

This was initially planned without the udon, yet when we tested it, I was thinking how much I'd love to have some noodles in there. It may seem like it would be better suited to rice, but it's honestly 10 out of 10 with the udon!

GET AHEAD Roast the cashews and make the dressing in advance.

1] Roast the cashews (*see page 22*). Whisk up the dressing in a large mixing bowl.

2] Place a frying pan over a medium-high heat and add the oil. Peel and finely grate the garlic and ginger directly into the pan. Cook for 2 minutes, then add the spices and toast for 2 minutes until fragrant. Stir into the dressing. Peel the carrots and parsnips, then use the peeler to peel them into ribbons directly into the bowl. Massage them so that they're well coated in the dressing – *this will soften them a bit.*

3] Put the udon noodles into a bowl, cover with boiling water and set aside for 2 minutes. Drain and rinse with cold water until completely cooled, then drain well. Add to the bowl and toss.

4] Finely slice the spring onions and add them to the bowl. Pull the herb leaves from the stems and roughly chop, then add most to the bowl and season generously with salt and pepper. Add most of the roasted cashews. Finely grate in the zest of the lime and squeeze in the juice, then toss to combine. Transfer to a platter or plates and top with the remaining cashews and herbs.

Chaat

SERVES 4
TIME 50 mins
VIBE Easy-peasy

NICE ON THE SIDE
Curries or spiced joints of meat

SALAD PARTY?
Serve with Spiced Chicken with Minty Yogurt (*see* page 108)

1 tablespoon ginger and garlic paste

2 tablespoons curry powder

1 teaspoon ground turmeric

2 teaspoons garam masala

2 teaspoons ground coriander

1 large cauliflower

2 × 400g (14oz) cans of chickpeas

450g (1lb) paneer

1 small bunch (about 30g/1oz) coriander

1 small bunch (about 30g/1oz) mint

80g (2¾oz) pomegranate seeds

1 lime

80g (2¾oz) natural yogurt

salt and pepper

DRESSING

Lemon & Olive Oil (*see* page 16), swapping the lemon juice for lime juice

TOPPERS

2–3 tablespoons mango chutney

a few of the pomegranate seeds (*see* above)

a few of the herb leaves (*see* above)

There so many chaats I love that I really struggled to choose my fave. In the end, I went with this cauliflower and pomegranate number with added paneer! It hits the spot every time I make it. If you can get your hands on some sev – that spiced crunchy noodle Indian snack – sprinkle it all over the top.

SUBS Ⓥ Swap the paneer for cubes of firm tofu and use coconut yogurt or other vegan alternative.

GET AHEAD Make the dressing in advance.

1] Preheat the oven to 220°C/200°C fan/425°F/Gas Mark 7. Whisk up the dressing in a large mixing bowl, then add the ginger and garlic paste along with the ground spices and mix together well.

2] Cut the cauliflower into florets and spread out in a roasting tray. Drizzle with half of the dressing and toss well. Roast for 20 minutes. Meanwhile, drain and rinse the chickpeas, then drain well and pat them dry with kitchen paper. Remove the tray from the oven, add the chickpeas and another tablespoon of the dressing and roast for another 10–15 minutes until the cauliflower is charred. Set aside to cool a little.

3] Heat a frying pan over a high heat. Pat the paneer dry, then cut into 2cm (¾-inch) cubes. Add to the remaining dressing in the bowl and toss to coat, then transfer to the hot pan and fry for 4 minutes, turning occasionally, until charred on all sides. Add to the cauliflower and chickpeas in the tray. Pull the herb leaves from the stems and add most to the tray along with most of the pomegranate seeds. Finely grate in the zest of the lime and squeeze in the juice, then toss well, taste and season well with salt and pepper.

4] Transfer the salad to a platter and drizzle with the yogurt. Finish with the mango chutney and remaining pomegranate seeds and herb leaves.

Fitzroy

SERVES 4
TIME 30 mins
VIBE Showing off a bit

NICE ON THE SIDE
Green salad and warm
crusty bread

SALAD PARTY?
Serve with Courgette & White
Bean (*see* page 28)

1 heaped tablespoon curry
powder
½ × 50g (1¾oz) can of anchovy
fillets in olive oil
100g (3½oz) almonds
2 cauliflowers (about 800g/1lb
12oz in total)
4 eggs
200g (7oz) crab meat,
preferably half brown and half
white (such as Fifty Fifty Crab)
1 small bunch (about 30g/1oz)
flat leaf parsley
3 tablespoons capers
1 lemon
salt and pepper

DRESSING
Lemon & Olive Oil (*see* page 16),
plus 2 heaped tablespoons
mayonnaise

TOPPERS
a little of the parsley
(*see* above)
a few of the almonds
(*see* above)

I ate a version of this salad at one of my favourite restaurants in the world – Fitzroy in Fowey. I loved it so much that I couldn't wait to try and create a version at home. I hope my version does their incredible dish justice.

SUBS **V** **VE** Swap the crab meat for canned chickpeas, omit the anchovies and also omit the eggs for vegans. Use vegan mayonnaise in the dressing

GET AHEAD Make the dressing and roast the nuts in advance. Macerate the cauliflower up to 3 hours in advance (preferably).

1] Whisk up the dressing including the mayo in a large mixing bowl, then mix in the curry powder. Drain and finely chop the anchovies, then add to the bowl. Roast the almonds (*see* page 22).

2] Remove the leaves from the cauliflowers. Slice the cauliflowers into quarters through the root, then use a mandolin or very sharp knife to slice as finely as you possibly can. Add to the dressing, then mix really well and set aside to soften.

3] Bring a pan of water to the boil, add the eggs and cook for 6 minutes. Drain, then tap them on a surface to crack the shell a little. Add to a bowl and cover with very cold water.

4] Add the crab meat to the cauliflower in the bowl. Roughly chop the parsley leaves and almonds and add most to the bowl. Add the capers and stir well. Halve the lemon and add the juice of one half to the salad, then taste and season generously with salt and pepper. Cut the remaining lemon half into wedges to serve.

5] Transfer the salad to bowls or a platter. Shell and halve the eggs, then top the salad with the egg halves, the remaining parsley and almonds. Finish with black pepper and serve with the lemon wedges.

Katsu Chicken

SERVES 4
TIME 1 hour
VIBE Not too tricky

NICE ON THE SIDE
Fried soy greens or
miso green salad

SALAD PARTY?
Serve with Curried Carrot &
Parsnip Udon (page 100) and/or
Grilled Nutty Greens (page 143)

thumb-sized chunk of fresh
  root ginger
3 garlic cloves
1 tablespoon curry powder
pinch of chilli powder
4 skinless chicken breasts
250g (9oz) jasmine or basmati
  rice
2 teaspoons ground turmeric
500ml (18fl oz) water
4 spring onions
1 cucumber
1 small bunch (about 30g/1oz)
  coriander
1 lime, or to taste
soy sauce, to taste

DRESSING
Chilli & Lime (see page 19)

TOPPERS
50g (1¾oz) Toasted
  Breadcrumbs with coconut
  (see page 25), optional
a few of the coriander leaves
  (see above)

If you have time, do prepare the coconut breadcrumbs, as they
make this feel a bit like you're using breaded chicken.

SUBS **V** **VE** Swap the chicken for firm tofu – slice and toss in the
marinade, then fry for 2–3 minutes until crispy and charred.

GET AHEAD Make the dressing in advance. Marinate the chicken
up to 24 hours in advance in an airtight container in the refrigerator.
Make the toasted breadcrumbs in advance.

1] Whisk up the dressing in a large mixing bowl, then pour half of it
into a separate bowl to act as the marinade base.

2] Peel the ginger and garlic, then grate both into the marinade bowl
along with the curry and chilli powders. Mix well. Add the chicken to
the bowl and toss to coat, then cover and leave to marinate in the
refrigerator while you prepare the rice.

3] Rinse the rice in a sieve until the water runs clear. Put into a
saucepan, add the turmeric along with a big pinch of salt, then pour
in the measured water. Bring to the boil, cover with a lid, reduce the
heat to a very gentle simmer and cook for 10 minutes. Remove from
the heat and set aside with the lid on for 5 minutes. Meanwhile, make
the toasted breadcrumbs, if using.

4] Heat a frying pan over a medium-high heat. Once hot, add the
chicken with all the marinade and cook for 2 minutes on each side
until golden, then reduce the heat to medium-low, cover with a lid
and cook for 10 minutes. Set aside with the lid on for 5 minutes.

5] Rinse the rice with cold water until cooled to room temperature
and drain well, then add to the bowl of dressing. Finely slice the spring
onions and cut the cucumber into half moons, then add to the rice.
Roughly chop most of the coriander, then add to the bowl. Toss, taste

and add a little lime juice or soy sauce to taste. Transfer to plates or a platter.

6] Slice the chicken, then place on top of the rice. Sprinkle with the coconut breadcrumbs, if using. Finish with the remaining coriander leaves. Slice the lime into wedges and serve on the side.

Spiced Chicken with Minty Yogurt

SERVES 4
TIME 35 mins
VIBE Showing off a little

NICE ON THE SIDE
Coconut rice and naan bread

SALAD PARTY?
Serve with Bombay Potato (*see page 94*) and/or Curried Carrot & Parsnip Udon (*see page 100*)

2 teaspoons dried mint

1 tablespoon cumin seeds

1 tablespoon ground coriander

1 tablespoon curry powder

6 boneless, skinless chicken thighs

75g (2¾oz) raisins

1 green chilli

120g (4¼oz) natural yogurt

juice of 1 lime (about 1 tablespoon)

2 Romaine lettuces

1 large cucumber (or 2 smaller)

2 avocados

½ bunch (about 50g/1¾oz) spring onions

½ small bunch (about 15g/½oz) coriander

½ small bunch (about 15g/½oz) mint

salt and pepper

DRESSING

Lemon & Olive Oil (*see page 16*), swapping the lemon juice for lime juice – *add the finely grated zest for an extra kick!*

TOPPERS

3–4 tablespoons crispy onions or 50g (1¾oz) cashew nuts

Spiced chicken with cooling yogurt and cucumber – nothing to complain about here.

SUBS Ⓥ ⓋⒻ Swap the chicken for firm tofu, and use coconut yogurt for vegans.

GET AHEAD Make the dressing and, if using, roast the cashews in advance. Make the minty yogurt up to 2 days in advance and store in an airtight container in the refrigerator.

1] Whisk up the dressing in a large mixing bowl. Add 1 teaspoon of the dried mint. Heat a dry frying pan over a medium-high heat, add the spices and toast for a minute until fragrant, then add to the dressing. Transfer 2 tablespoons of the dressing to another bowl with the chicken and toss to coat. Cover and leave to marinate in the refrigerator while you prepare the rest of the salad.

2] Add the raisins to the large bowl with the remaining dressing. Finely chop the chilli and add to the bowl. Roast the cashews, if using (*see page 22*).

3] Mix the yogurt with the remaining dried mint. Add half of the lime juice and season with salt and pepper. Loosen to a drizzling consistency with a splash of water and set aside.

4] Shred the lettuces – *if they look at all dirty, wash in iced water and spin to dry* – and add to the bowl. Cut the cucumber into 2cm (¾-inch) chunks and add to the bowl. Halve each avocado and remove the stone, then cut a criss-cross pattern into the cut sides of each half and use a spoon to scoop out the cubes into the bowl – *this technique makes cutting avocados into cubes both easy and mess free!* Finely

slice the spring onions and add to the bowl. Pull the herb leaves from the stems and add most of them to the bowl. Cover and refrigerate – *don't toss yet!*

5] Remove the chicken from the refrigerator. Heat a frying pan over a high heat, add the chicken and cook for 3–4 minutes on each side until charred and cooked through. Set aside on a chopping board.

6] Remove the salad from the refrigerator, toss and season well, then taste and add the extra lime juice if needed. Transfer to bowls or a platter.

7] Slice the chicken and arrange on top of the salad. Add the minty yogurt and the remaining herbs, then sprinkle with crispy onions or the roasted cashews.

Spiced Aubergine & Lentil

SERVES 4
TIME 30 mins
VIBE Not too tricky

NICE ON THE SIDE
Slow-cooked meats or falafels
and pitta breads

SALAD PARTY?
Serve with Fig & Feta (*see* page
62) and/or Za'atar Fattoush
(*see* page 95)

2 large aubergines

100g (3½oz) walnuts

2 lemons

4 tablespoons olive oil

2 × 250g (9oz) pouches ready-
cooked Puy lentils

1 small bunch (about 30g/1oz)
flat leaf parsley

2 garlic cloves

2 teaspoons cumin seeds

2 teaspoons black mustard
seeds

2 teaspoons ground coriander

salt and pepper

DRESSING

Tahini (*see* page 16)

TOPPERS

a little of the parsley
(*see* above)

a few of the walnuts
(*see* above)

The real trick with aubergines is to always dry-fry or char them before oiling them up – this way they don't just absorb all the oil like a sponge before they cook through.

GET AHEAD Cook the aubergines the day before and store in an airtight container in the refrigerator. Roast the nuts and make the dressing in advance.

1] Roughly chop the aubergines into 3cm (1¼-inch) chunks. Preheat the grill to its highest setting. Spread the aubergine chunks out on a baking tray, sprinkle with salt and slide under the grill for 10–12 minutes until charred and collapsed.

2] Meanwhile, roast the walnuts (*see* page 22), and make the dressing.

3] Halve the lemons and squeeze the juice from 3 halves into a large mixing bowl. Add 2 tablespoons of the olive oil and whisk together. Add the lentils. Pull the parsley leaves from the stems and finely chop, then finely chop the roasted walnuts. Add most of the parsley and walnuts to the bowl, season well with salt and pepper and toss to combine. Cut the remaining lemon half into wedges.

4] Heat the remaining oil in a large frying pan over a medium heat. peel and grate the garlic directly into the pan and then add the spices and cook for 2 minutes. Add the aubergine chunks and stir, ensuring it's well coated. Cook for a further minute then add the aubergine mixture to the mixing bowl with the lemon and toss well.

5] Transfer to a platter or bowls and drizzle with the dressing. Top with the remaining parsley and walnuts and serve.

ON THIS PAGE Tabbouleh (see page 39), Spiced Aubergine & Lentil (see page 111), Za'atar Fattoush (see page 95)

Wintery

'I'd like to really push the argument that salads are not just for spring and summer. Some of my favourite salads use up all the ingredients that you can only really get your hands on in the autumn or winter. For those of us that want to eat salad as much in November as in July, the next few pages are packed with really delicious options that don't leave you heading out into the cold feeling like you could have done with something a bit more substantial. Summer salads are in fact, SO last season.'

Winter Panzanella

SERVES 4
TIME 45 mins
VIBE Easy-peasy

NICE ON THE SIDE
Hummus, or stuffed and roasted squash or belly pork for an alternative Sunday roast

SALAD PARTY?
Serve with Carrot, Date & Puy Lentil (*see* page 126) and/or Squash & Freekeh (*see* page 134)

4–6 raw beetroots or 2 × approx. 250g (9oz) packets ready-cooked beetroots – *not in vinegar!*
Garlic 'n' Herb Croutons (*see* page 23)
1 large cauliflower
2 tablespoons olive oil
1 tablespoon za'atar
80g (7¾oz) pomegranate seeds (plus any juice in the packet)
1 teaspoon sumac
½ small bunch (about 15g/½oz) flat leaf parsley
½ small bunch (about 15g/½oz) dill
3 tablespoons capers
200g (7oz) halloumi cheese
salt and pepper

DRESSING
Honey & Mustard (*see* page 16)

TOPPERS
30g (1oz) sesame seeds

Photographed on page 114

If you love a summery panzanella (aka a salad with big fat chunks of crunchy bread), then this can seamlessly take its place in winter months.

SUBS Ⓥ Swap the halloumi for firm tofu or tempeh cut into cubes and the honey in the dressing for sugar or maple syrup.

GET AHEAD Make the croutons and dressing in advance.

1] If using raw beetroot, preheat the oven to 240°C/220°C fan/475°F/Gas Mark 9. Wrap each beetroot in foil, place in a roasting tray and roast for 1–1½ hours, depending on their size. Remove from the oven, unwrap and set aside until cool enough to handle before peeling. Make the croutons.

2] Turn down the oven (or preheat) to 200°C/180°C fan/400°F/Gas Mark 6. Remove the leaves from the cauliflower and add to a roasting tray. Roughly chop the cauliflower into florets, add to the tray and drizzle with the oil, then sprinkle over the za'atar, season well with salt and pepper and toss. Roast for 25–30 minutes until charred and softened.

3] Meanwhile, toast the sesame seeds (*see* page 22). Whisk up the dressing in a large mixing bowl. Roughly chop the beetroots into wedges and add to the bowl.

4] Add the cauliflower and pomegranate seeds along with the sumac. Pull the herb leaves from the stems and roughly chop, then and add to the bowl along with the croutons and capers. Gently toss.

5] Heat a nonstick frying pan over a high heat. Cut the halloumi into 2cm (¾-inch) cubes, add to the pan and cook for 3–5 minutes, turning as they brown on each side. Add to the bowl and give everything a final toss – *the bread should be a little softened in the juices.* Transfer to a big platter and sprinkle with toasted sesame seeds.

Sprout, Sesame & Apple

SERVES 4
TIME 15 mins
VIBE Easy-peasy

NICE ON THE SIDE
Leftover turkey noodles!

SALAD PARTY?
Serve with Cauli Wedge (*see* page 139) and/or Celeriac, Barley & Walnut (*see* pages 128–129)

3 tablespoons sesame seeds
500g (1lb 2oz) Brussels sprouts
2 apples
1 small bunch (about 30g/1oz) coriander
1 red chilli

DRESSING

Miso & Lime (*see* page 19), plus 1 tablespoon tahini, plus more lime juice, to taste

TOPPERS

a few of the coriander leaves (*see* above)

Let me set the scene. It's Boxing Day, you're using the leftovers to make some kind of spicy turkey noodle dish and you want a salad on the side. Enter this guy. It's also really well suited to any of the other wintery salads in this chapter as a lighter, sharper accompaniment.

GET AHEAD Make the dressing in advance.

1] Toast the sesame seeds (*see* page 22).

2] Whisk up the dressing including the tahini, adding a little water to loosen it. Taste and add a little more lime juice if needed.

3] Slice the sprouts and put them in a large serving bowl. Core the apples and cut into matchsticks. Pull the coriander leaves from the stems, roughly chop most of them and add to the bowl. Add the toasted sesame seeds. Finely slice the chilli and add to the bowl. Add the dressing and toss well. Top with the remaining coriander leaves.

Kale Chicken Caesar

SERVES 4
TIME 30 mins
VIBE Not too tricky

NICE ON THE SIDE
Potatoes or roasted winter veg

SALAD PARTY?
Serve with Radicchio & Beetroot
(*see* page 132) and/or Squash &
Freekeh (*see* page 134)

2 skinless chicken breasts
1 tablespoon olive oil
200g (7oz) kale
juice of ½ lemon (about
    1 tablespoon)
½ × 50g (1¾oz) can of anchovy
    fillets in olive oil
2 tablespoons capers
salt and pepper

DRESSING
Caesar or Cheat's Caesar
    (*see* page 18)

TOPPERS
50g (1¾oz) Toasted
    Breadcrumbs (*see* page 25)
30g (1oz) Parmesan cheese

Yes, 2 Caesars because, while the OG is my favourite salad ever, sometimes you need a little wintery option with breadcrumbs and chicken, and copious amounts of anchovies ofc.

SUBS Ⓥ Swap the chicken for firm tofu, and omit the anchovies and replace with extra capers; omit the anchovies and use a vegetarian hard cheese in the dressings and for topping.
ⓋⒺ As for Ⓥ but use the cheat's Caesar dressing with vegan mayonnaise and Parmesan-style 'cheese', omitting the anchovies; omit the Parmesan topper.

GET AHEAD Make the dressing and the toasted breadcrumbs in advance.

1] Make the dressing.

2] Heat a large frying pan over a medium heat. Rub the chicken with the oil and season well with salt and pepper, then add to the frying pan and cook for 4 minutes on each side until golden. Use tongs to remove from the pan and set aside. Take the pan off the heat and leave to cool for a minute, then use it to fry your breadcrumbs for the topper.

3] Put the kale into a large mixing bowl. Add the lemon juice and use your hands to firmly massage it into the kale for a few minutes until it visibly softens. Stir in 3–4 tablespoons of the dressing and toss to combine, then taste and add a little more if you like. Drain the anchovies and add to the bowl with the capers. Toss again, then transfer to bowls.

4] Slice the chicken breasts and lay on top of the salad. Finish with the toasted breadcrumbs and grate over the Parmesan.

Winter Citrus

SERVES 4
TIME 30 mins
VIBE Easy-peasy

NICE ON THE SIDE
Glazed short ribs or slow-cooked meats, or ragu with pappardelle or wintery stews.

SALAD PARTY?
Serve with Beetroot & Chickpea (*see* page 98) and/or Squash & Freekeh (*see* page 134).

75g (⅔oz) walnuts
50g (1¾oz) dried cranberries
100g (3½oz) pitted black olives
1 small red onion
3 clementines
2 oranges
1 pink grapefruit
2 heads of red chicory
1 head of radicchio

DRESSING

Honey & Mustard (*see* page 16), plus 1 tablespoon pomegranate molasses (optional)

TOPPERS

a few of the walnuts (*see* above)

This guy is the perfect accompaniment to a rich wintery meal that needs a little something extra. It looks pretty darn great too.

SUBS 🅥 Swap the honey in the dressing for sugar or maple syrup.

GET AHEAD Roast the walnuts and make the dressing in advance. Add the dried cranberries, olives and red onion to the dressing up to 3 hours in advance.

1] Roast the walnuts (*see* page 22).

2] Whisk up the dressing including the pomegranate molasses in a large mixing bowl, then add the dried cranberries. Halve the olives, peel and finely slice the red onion and add both to the dressing, then set aside.

3] Peel all of the citrus fruit and remove as much of the white pith as possible. Then either slice between the membranes to release the segments or cut into rounds. Add to the bowl.

4] Separate the leaves of the chicory and radicchio and add to the bowl. Add most of the walnuts, breaking them up with your hands as you go. Give everything a gentle toss, then transfer to a platter. Sprinkle with the remaining roasted walnuts.

Mushroom & Barley

SERVES 4
TIME 50 mins
VIBE showing off a little

NICE ON THE SIDE
Slow-roasted pork or lamb
shoulder or roasted winter veg
with feta

SALAD PARTY?
Serve with Winter Citrus (see
page 121) and/or Pumpkin &
Burrata (see page 184)

350g (12oz) pearl barley
850ml (1½ pints) boiling water
3 tablespoons olive oil
1 lemon
80g (2¾oz) rocket
3 tablespoons capers
½ small bunch (about 15g/½oz)
  tarragon
½ small bunch (about 15g/½oz)
  dill
750g (1lb 10oz) mushrooms
  – I use a mixture of wild
  mushrooms
40g (1½oz) unsalted butter
2 garlic cloves
1 tablespoon fennel seeds
1 tablespoon thyme leaves
salt and pepper

DRESSING
Yogurt (see page 16)

TOPPERS
30g (1oz) pumpkin seeds
a few of the herb leaves
  (see above)

My mates Suzy and Tish made me a version of this perfect autumnal salad and I was immediately hooked, I'm sure you will be too.

SUBS ⓥⒺ Use vegan yogurt and maple syrup instead of honey in the dressing, and swap the butter for olive oil.

GET AHEAD Cook and rinse the barley until completely cooled up to 2 days in advance, then store in an airtight container in the refrigerator. Make the dressing and toast the pumpkin seeds in advance.

1] Rinse the barley until the water runs clear. Put into a large saucepan, cover with the measured boiling water and add a big pinch of salt. Place over a medium-high heat and bring to the boil. Reduce the heat to a simmer, cover and simmer for about 30 minutes or until the barley is cooked through. If the water has been absorbed before the barley is cooked through, simply add more and keep cooking. Drain and rinse with cool water to wash away the starch, drain and put in a large mixing bowl.

2] Make the dressing and toast the pumpkin seeds (see page 22).

3] Add the oil to the barley along with the zest and juice of the lemon, then add the rocket and capers along with most of the herb leaves. Toss, taste and season generously with salt and pepper.

4] Roughly chop the mushrooms into similar-sized pieces. Put the butter in a large frying pan and place over a medium heat. Once it has melted, keep whisking it as it foams and then turns brown and smells like nuts – about 4 minutes. Increase the heat, add the mushrooms along with a big pinch of salt and fry for 10–15 minutes, stirring regularly, until golden. Peel and slice the garlic then add to the pan along with the fennel seeds and thyme and cook for another 2 minutes.

5] Transfer the barley mixture to a platter and top with the mushrooms, the yogurt dressing, remaining herb leaves and toasted pumpkin seeds.

Leeks & Cannellini Beans

SERVES 4
TIME 45 mins
VIBE Not too tricky

NICE ON THE SIDE
Poached chicken or pan-fried fish

SALAD PARTY?
Serve with Radicchio & Beetroot (page 132) and/or Blue Cheese, Bacon & Celery (page 200)

6 leeks
olive oil
1–2 shallots, depending on their size
90g (3¼oz) pitted green olives
½ × 50g (1¾oz) can anchovy fillets in olive oil (optional)
2 × 400g (14oz) cans cannellini beans
½ small bunch (about 15g/½oz) flat leaf parsley
½ small bunch (about 15g/½oz) tarragon – *if you can't find tarragon, just use more parsley*
4 tablespoons capers
salt and pepper

DRESSING
Honey & Mustard (*see* page 16)

TOPPERS
50g (1¾oz) blanched hazelnuts or walnuts, or Savoury Granola (*see* page 24)
a few of the herbs (*see* above)

Grilled leeks are always incredible, but piled on top of these beans and topped with the green olives, they really get their moment.

SUBS **V** Omit the anchovies. **VE** Omit the anchovies and the savoury granola, and swap the honey in the dressing for sugar or maple syrup.

GET AHEAD Make the dressing and roast the nuts or make the savoury granola in advance.

1] Roast the nuts (*see* page 22) or make the savoury granola. Turn the oven up (or preheat) to 220°C/200°C fan/425°F/Gas Mark 7. Line a roasting tray with foil. Trim the tops of the leeks and remove any of the thick outer layers, then slice in half lengthways – *but don't remove the root!* Place in the roasting tray, drizzle with a little olive oil and season well with salt and pepper. Loosely cover with another piece of foil and roast for 15–20 minutes until completely soft.

2] Meanwhile, whisk up the dressing in a mixing bowl. Peel and finely chop the shallots and halve the olives. Drain and finely chop the anchovies, if using, then add all to the dressing.

3] Turn on the grill to high. Remove the leeks from the oven and take off the top sheet of foil. Slide them under the grill and grill for 10 minutes until blackened and charred.

4] Drain and rinse the beans, then drain well and put in a large mixing bowl. Add half of the dressing mixture. Pull the herb leaves from most of the stems and finely chop, then add to the bowl. Add the capers and toss well, then transfer the salad to a platter.

5] Top with the leeks, then drizzle with the remaining dressing. Roughly chop the nuts, if using. Sprinkle over the nuts or Savoury Granola, along with the remaining herb sprigs and add a crack of black pepper.

Carrot, Date & Puy Lentil

SERVES 4
TIME 50 mins
VIBE Showing off a little

NICE ON THE SIDE
Sharp wintery salads or a roasted joint of beef for an alternative roast dinner!

SALAD PARTY?
Serve with Winter Citrus (*see page 121*) and/or Cauli Wedge (*see page 139*)

650g (1lb 7oz) small or
   baby carrots
1 tablespoon olive oil
1 tablespoon cumin seeds
1 tablespoon ras el hanout
200g (7oz) natural yogurt
2 tablespoons tahini
2 × 250g (9oz) pouches of
   ready-cooked Puy lentils
½ small bunch (about 15g/½oz)
   mint
½ small bunch (about 15g/½oz)
   flat leaf parsley
salt and pepper

DRESSING
Honey & Mustard (*see page 16*), swapping the honey for 2–3 pitted dates
cider or white wine vinegar, to taste

TOPPERS
30g (1oz) pine nuts (optional)
30g (1oz) sesame seeds (optional)
a few of the herb leaves (*see above*)
big pinch of chilli powder

To my mind, carrots are either best raw (preferably served with hummus in a ratio that really screams that the carrots are merely a vessel) OR like this – hard roasted, sticky, sweet and a bit spicy.

SUBS Ⓥ Use vegan yogurt – I use coconut yogurt.

GET AHEAD Roast the pine nuts and toast the sesame seeds, if using, and make the dressing in advance.

1] Roast the pine nuts; toast the sesame seeds (*see page 22*), if using.

2] Turn the oven up (or preheat) to 200°C/180°C fan/400°F/Gas Mark 6. Halve any chunkier carrots lengthways, then add them all to a large roasting tray with the oil and toss to coat. Sprinkle with the cumin seeds and ras el hanout along with a big pinch of salt and pepper, then roast for 40 minutes or until charred and soft.

3] Meanwhile, make the dressing. Put all the ingredients including 2 of the dates into a mini chopper or blender and blitz until smooth. Season with salt and pepper, then taste and add a little more vinegar to taste – you want it to be balanced between sweetness and acidity. Add the final date if you prefer it a little sweeter and blitz to combine.

4] Whisk the yogurt with the tahini in a bowl, adding a splash of water if it seizes – *you want it to be thick enough to spread across a plate.*

5] Once the carrots are cooked, remove from the oven. Add the lentils to the roasting tray. Pull the herb leaves from the stems and add most of them to the tray. Add the dressing along with a splash of boiling water, and gently toss everything to combine.

6] Spread the tahini yogurt on to a large plate and top with the carrots and lentils. Sprinkle over the remaining herb leaves, and the toasted pine nuts and sesame seeds if using, and finish with the chilli powder.

Celeriac, Barley & Walnut

SERVES 4
TIME 50 mins
VIBE Showing off a little

NICE ON THE SIDE
Roast joints of meat

SALAD PARTY?
Serve with Winter Citrus (*see page 121*) and/or Cauli Wedge (*see page 139*)

75g (2¾oz) walnuts
1 large celeriac
1 tablespoon fennel seeds
3 tablespoons olive oil
1 garlic bulb
200g (7oz) pearl barley
500ml (18fl oz) boiling water
juice of ½ lemon (about 1
    tablespoon)
3–4 pickled walnuts (optional)
1 small bunch (about 30g/1oz)
    flat leaf parsley
1 small bunch (about 30g/1oz)
    tarragon
80g (2¾oz) raisins or sultanas
salt and pepper

DRESSING
Tahini (*see page 16*)

TOPPERS
a few of the walnuts
    (*see above*)
a few of the herb leaves
    (*see above*)

Celeriac is the most underrated root veg. I'm pretty sure it's because it looks a bit gnarly and high-maintenance, but chop it in half, peel off the skin and make the most of it. These celeriac chunks, roasted and tossed with all the nutty sharp goodness of the rest of this salad, are here to show you just what a winner celeriac can be.

SUBS Ⓥ Use vegan yogurt and maple syrup instead of honey in the dressing.

GET AHEAD Roast the walnuts in advance. Cook and rinse the barley up to 2 days in advance, then store in an airtight container in the refrigerator. Make the dressing in advance.

1] Roast the walnuts (*see page 22*).

2] Increase the oven temperature (or preheat) to 200°C/180°C fan/400°F/Gas Mark 6. Peel and chop the celeriac into 3cm (1¼-inch) chunks. Spread out in a large roasting tray, sprinkle with the fennel seeds and drizzle with 1½ tablespoons of the oil, then season with salt and pepper and toss well. Wrap the garlic bulb in foil, then snuggle into the corner of the pan. Roast for 30–40 minutes, tossing regularly, until the celeriac is charred and the garlic bulb totally soft.

3] Meanwhile, rinse the barley until the water runs clear. Put into a saucepan, cover with the measured boiling water and add a big pinch of salt. Place over a medium-high heat and bring to the boil. Reduce the heat to a simmer, cover with a lid and bubble away for about 30 minutes until all the liquid has been absorbed and the barley is cooked though but with a very slight bite. *If the water has been absorbed before the barley has cooked through, simply add more* *and keep cooking.* Drain and rinse with cool water to wash away the starch, then drain well. If using, chop the pickled walnuts into half moons.

4] Mix up the dressing and loosen with a little water to make it a drizzling consistency.

5] Remove the garlic from the roasting tray, then add the barley to the tray with the remaining oil, the lemon juice, chopped pickled walnuts, if using, and most of the roasted walnuts. Pull the herb leaves from the stems and add most of them to the tray. Add the raisins or sultanas. Unwrap the garlic bulb and squeeze the garlic cloves from their skins into the barley mixture – *if they're too hot to handle, use the back of spoon to squish out.* Then toss everything together well, taste and season.

6] Transfer the salad to a plate, drizzle with the dressing and top with the remaining roasted walnuts and herb leaves. Serve with any remaining dressing for people to add at the table.

Radicchio & Beetroot

SERVES 4
TIME 30 mins
VIBE Feeling a little more fancy

NICE ON THE SIDE
Smoked mackerel, wintery stews
or roasted joints of meat

SALAD PARTY?
Serve with Cauli Wedge (*see*
page 139) and/or Squash &
Freekeh (*see* page 134)

approx. 2x 250g (9oz) packets
  of ready-cooked beetroots –
  not in vinegar!
1 head of radicchio
2 heads of red chicory
50g (1¾oz) pitted black olives
  (optional)
75g (2¾oz) ricotta salata
  (salted ricotta), or pecorino
½ small bunch (about 15g/½oz)
  dill
½ small bunch (about 15g/½oz)
  chives
salt and pepper

DRESSING
Honey & Mustard (*see* page
  16), swapping the mustard for
  horseradish sauce

TOPPERS
50g (1¾oz) Savoury Granola
  (*see* page 24), or blanched
  hazelnuts, or pecan nuts
50g (1¾oz) pickled radishes
  (*see* page 23)
a few of the herbs (*see* above)
a little of the cheese
  (*see* above)

Let this beetroot beauty shine by placing it centre stage in the middle of the table – you only have to look at it to know that's what it was born to do.

SUBS Ⓥ Use a vegetarian hard cheese. ⓋⒺ Use a vegan Parmesan-style 'cheese', swap the honey in the dressing for sugar or maple syrup and omit the savoury granola.

GET AHEAD Make the savoury granola or roast the nuts, and make the pickled radishes and dressing in advance.

1] Make the savoury granola or roast the nuts (*see* page 22). Make the pickled radishes.

2] Whisk up the dressing in a large mixing bowl. Cut a small snip in one of the beetroot packets and pour 2 tablespoons of the juice into a small jug or mug. Drain off the rest of the juice, then slice all the remining beetroots into wedges and add to the bowl.

3] Separate the leaves of the radicchio and chicory and add to the bowl. If using, halve the olives and add to the bowl. Use a peeler to shave most of the cheese directly into the bowl. Pull the dill leaves from the stems and finely slice the chives, then add most of the herbs to the bowl. Toss everything together and season with salt and pepper.

4] Transfer to a large plate, sprinkle over the remaining herbs and shave over the remaining cheese. Top with the pickled radishes and savoury granola or roasted nuts.

Squash & Freekeh

SERVES 4
TIME 50 mins
VIBE Showing off a little

NICE ON THE SIDE
Spatchcocked chicken or roasted pork belly

SALAD PARTY?
Serve with Cauli Wedge (see page 139) and/or Halloumi & Sesame (see page 192)

1 large butternut squash (about 800g/1lb 12oz)

2 tablespoons olive oil

2 teaspoons ground coriander

2 teaspoons cumin seeds

300g (10½oz) freekeh

600ml (20fl oz) boiling water

1–2 tablespoons harissa

1 small bunch (about 30g/1oz) dill

1 lemon

salt and pepper

100g (3½oz) feta cheese, to serve (optional)

DRESSING
Green Sauce (see page 17) or Lemon & Olive Oil (see page 16)

TOPPERS
50g (1¾oz) blanched hazelnuts

a few of the dill leaves (see above)

50g (1¾oz) pomegranate seeds (optional)

I really begin to crave this kind of salad as soon as the days start getting shorter, the kind of food that makes you look forward to the wintery months. Go wild with the green sauce on the top.

SUBS Ⓥ Use vegan feta-style 'cheese' or omit.

GET AHEAD Roast the hazelnuts in advance. Cook and rinse the freekeh up to 2 days in advance, then store in an airtight container in the refrigerator. Make the dressing in advance.

1] Roast the hazelnuts (see page 22). Turn up the oven (or preheat) to 240°C/220°C/475°F/Gas Mark 9. Cut the squash in half vertically, deseed and slice into wedges, keeping the skin on. Pile on to your largest baking tray. Drizzle with the oil and scatter with the ground coriander and cumin seeds, then season generously with salt and pepper and toss. Roast for 30–40 minutes, turning the wedges over halfway through, until the squash is totally soft. *If it's still firm, roast for another 10 minutes.*

2] Meanwhile, put the freekeh into a large saucepan and cover with the measured boiling water. Season well, place over a medium-high heat and bring to the boil. Reduce the heat to a simmer, cover with a lid and cook for 10 minutes, *If all the water has been absorbed before the freekeh is cooked through, simply add a splash more water and keep cooking until it's ready.* Drain and rinse with cold water to wash away the starch, then tip into a large mixing bowl.

3] Make the dressing and add half of it to the bowl of freekeh. Add the harissa along with most of the dill leaves, finely grate in the lemon zest and squeeze in the juice. Toss well, taste and season, then pile on to a platter or into bowls.

4] Top with the roasted squash and drizzle with the remaining dressing. Crush the hazelnuts and scatter on top along with the remaining dill. Crumble over the feta and sprinkle the pomegranate seeds, if using.

Sweet Potato & Miso

SERVES 4
TIME 50 mins
VIBE Not too tricky

NICE ON THE SIDE
Soy-glazed chicken or spicy fried greens

SALAD PARTY?
Serve with Spicy Chicken & Peanut (*see* page 78) and/or Spicy Noodle (*see* page 79)

4 sweet potatoes
2 tablespoons soy sauce
2 tablespoons sesame oil
2 garlic cloves
thumb-sized chunk of fresh root ginger
2 tablespoons sesame seeds
2 tablespoons roasted, salted peanuts
handful of mint leaves
handful of coriander leaves
25g (1oz) unsalted butter
1 tablespoon miso paste
1 lime

DRESSING
Tahini (*see* page 16)

TOPPERS
Nutty Sprinkle (*see* method)
1 green or red chilli
2 spring onions
a few of the herb leaves (*see* above)

A whole roast sweet potato drizzled with this exact dressing is up there with my favourite things to eat (pretty much anywhere at any time). So I've salad-ified that dish and added a miso nutty sprinkle.

SUBS Swap the butter for oil, but simply warm it and then add the remaining ingredients, as it won't turn brown like the butter.

GET AHEAD Make the dressing in advance.

1] Preheat the oven to 240°C/220°C fan/475°F/Gas Mark 9. Scrub the sweet potatoes if dirty, then cut into long, chunky wedges – *keeping them chunky means they won't turn too mushy!* Place on a large baking tray, drizzle with the soy sauce and sesame oil and toss well, then space them out as much as possible on the tray. Roast for 30–40 minutes, turning halfway through, until nice and charred on the outside.

2] Meanwhile, peel the garlic and ginger, then finely slice the garlic and cut the ginger into matchsticks. Toast the sesame seeds (*see* page 22), and roughly chop the peanuts. Finely chop around half of the herbs.

3] Put the butter in a large frying pan and place over a medium heat. Once the butter has melted, keep whisking it as it foams and then turns brown and smells like nuts – it takes about 4 minutes. Add the garlic and ginger along with the peanuts and sesame seeds and toast for a minute, then remove from the heat and stir in the miso and chopped herbs. Set aside.

4] Whisk up the dressing. Once the sweet potatoes are cooked, place on a large platter and drizzle with half of the dressing, then top with the miso butter mixture. Finely slice the chilli and spring onions and scatter over. Finish with the remaining herb leaves. Cut the lime into wedges and serve on the side. Serve with the remaining dressing for people to add at the table.

Cauli Wedge

SERVES 4

TIME 40 mins

VIBE Easy-peasy

NICE ON THE SIDE
Baked feta or lamb stew

SALAD PARTY?
Serve with Squash & Freekeh
(*see* page 134) and/or Halloumi &
Sesame (*see* page 192)

1 tablespoon za'atar

4 tablespoons olive oil

2 cauliflowers

1 red onion

1 lemon

½ small bunch (about 15g/½oz)
flat leaf parsley

½ small bunch (about 15g/½oz)
mint

100g (3½oz) pitted black olives

pepper

DRESSING

Yogurt (*see* page 16) – *Made
with thick Greek yogurt so it
spreads across the base of
the plate*

TOPPERS

30g (1 oz) sesame seeds

Big wedges of cauliflower piled onto a yogurt base and scattered
with black olives make this guy an undeniable crowd-pleaser. Best
served in the middle of the table surrounded by other wintery
salads.

GET AHEAD Toast the sesame seeds or roast the nuts, and make
the dressing in advance.

1] Toast the sesame seeds (*see* page 22).

2] Increase the oven temperature (or preheat) to 240°C/220°C
fan/475°F/Gas Mark 9. Mix the za'atar with the oil. Cut each of the
cauliflowers into 6–8 wedges through the root – *don't remove the
leaves, as they're going to be crispy and amazing!* Rub the wedges
all over with the za'atar oil. Place on a baking tray and roast for 25–35
minutes, or until charred and cooked through – *they might take a little
longer if your cauliflowers are particularly large.*

3] Peel and finely chop the red onion, then put in a mixing bowl.
Halve the lemon, then squeeze the juice of one half over the onion.
Pull the herb leaves from the stems and finely chop, then add to the
bowl and toss well. Finely chop the olives, add them to the bowl and
stir well. Cut the remaining lemon half into wedges.

4] Meanwhile, whisk up the dressing and spread across a large
platter. Pile the cauli wedges on top. Drizzle each wedge with the
dressing, then add the onion and herb mixture. Add the sesame
seeds and finish with a crack of black pepper.

Grilled

'You definitely don't need a barbecue to make these salads. However, if you've got one burning away, then definitely adjust the recipes to include whacking some of the veg (or meat) on the barbecue instead of in the pan or under the grill. These salads, for me, are the perfect summertime feasting recipes. Perfect for piling onto a platter to put in the middle of a table, hopefully on an evening warm enough to eat outside.'

Ratatouille

SERVES 4
TIME 30 mins
VIBE Easy-peasy

NICE ON THE SIDE
Pan-fried fish, roasted meats or
baked feta cheese

SALAD PARTY?
Serve with Potato Salad: The
Boiled One (*see* page 181) and/or
Chop Chop Feta (*see* page 185)

3 aubergines

1 red onion

1 teaspoon sugar

6 large juicy tomatoes

450g (1lb) jar roasted red
  peppers (about 350g/12oz
  drained weight)

2 courgettes

1 small bunch (about 30g/1oz)
  basil

1 teaspoon dried oregano

salt and pepper

DRESSING
Lemon & Olive Oil
  (*see* page 16)

TOPPERS
Garlic 'n' Herb Croutons
  (*see* page 23)

a few of the basil leaves
  (*see* above)

Parmesan cheese (optional)

Photographed on page 140

The thing that always used to bug me about ratatouille is the use of all the ingredients I crave on a summer's day, packed into a hot dish. So here we have it, same vibe, but in the form of a killer salad.

SUBS 🅥 🆅🅴 Omit the Parmesan topper.

GET AHEAD Make the croutons and dressing in advance.

1] Make the croutons.

2] Preheat the grill to its highest setting. Cut the aubergines into 3–4cm (1¼–1½-inch) chunks, spread out on a baking tray and season with salt. Slide under the grill and cook for about 10–12 minutes until soft and collapsing – *you may have to do this in 2 batches*. Set aside to cool to room temperature.

3] Meanwhile, whisk up the dressing in a large mixing bowl. Peel and finely slice the red onion, add to the bowl along with the sugar and set aside to lightly pickle. Cut the tomatoes into wedges, add to a seperate large mixing bowl with 1 teaspoon salt and toss, then set aside for 20 minutes.

4] Drain the roasted red peppers, then tear into the bowl of dressing and onion. Use a peeler to peel the courgettes into ribbons directly into the bowl. Pull the basil leaves from the stems and add most of them to the bowl along with the dried oregano. Drain the tomatoes and add them to the bowl, then toss to combine and season well with salt and pepper. Add the charred aubergines and gently toss – *to avoid crushing the chunks too much*.

5] Transfer to a platter and top with the croutons and the remaining basil leaves. Shave the Parmesan over the top, if using.

Grilled Nutty Greens

SERVES 4
TIME 20 mins
VIBE Easy-peasy

NICE ON THE SIDE
Crispy chilli squid or soy-glazed chicken thighs

SALAD PARTY?
Serve with Smashed Cucumber (*see* page 75) or Katsu Chicken (*see* page 106)

250g (9oz) asparagus spears
300g (10½oz) green beans
250g (9oz) Tenderstem broccoli spears
2 tablespoons sesame oil
1 small bunch (about 30g/1oz) coriander
100g (3½oz) roasted, salted peanuts
1 lime
salt and pepper

DRESSING
Miso & Lime (*see* page 19), plus 1 tablespoon peanut butter

TOPPERS
a few of the coriander leaves (*see* above)
a few of the peanuts (*see* above)

These nutty little guys are where it's at when you're looking for a salty hit alongside some noodles or fried rice. It also makes the very best barbecue side.

GET AHEAD Make the dressing in advance.

1] If using a charcoal barbecue, light the barbecue, then wait until it's no longer flaming and the coals are white. If not using a charcoal barbecue, heat a griddle pan over a high heat or preheat the grill to high. Snap the woody ends off the asparagus. Put in a large mixing bowl along with the beans, broccoli and sesame oil. Season well with salt and toss to coat. Transfer the greens to the barbecue or hot pan, or spread on a baking tray and slide under the grill. Cook for 10–15 minutes depending on the thickness of your greens, turning regularly, until charred and softened – *the cooking time will be much less if you're using a barbecue.*

2] Meanwhile, whisk up the dressing, including the peanut butter, in a large mixing bowl.

3] Once the greens are charred, add them to the dressing and toss well. Pull the coriander leaves from the stems and add most of them to the bowl, then roughly chop the peanuts and add most of them too. Toss, taste and season with salt and pepper.

4] Transfer the salad to a platter and top with the remaining coriander leaves and peanuts. Serve with wedges of lime.

Scallop & Sweetcorn

SERVES 4
TIME 35 mins
VIBE Showing off

NICE ON THE SIDE
Bread (*for sweeping up the oily juices*) or green salad

SALAD PARTY?
Serve with Courgette & Giant Couscous (*see* page 158) and/or Potato Salad: The Boiled One (*see* page 181)

4 corn on the cobs
45g (1½oz) unsalted butter
2 garlic cloves
80g (2¾oz) 'nduja or sliced
  chorizo sausage
olive oil, *if using chorizo*
500g (1lb 2oz) cherry tomatoes
1 small bunch (about 30g/1oz)
  flat leaf parsley
1 small bunch (about 30g/1oz)
  coriander
500g (1lb 2oz) raw scallops
1 lime
salt and pepper

DRESSING
Lemon & Olive Oil (*see* page
  16), swapping the lemon juice
  for lime juice

TOPPERS
a few of the herbs (*see* above)
crunchy corn (*this may be
  called snacking corn or
  corn nuts in your local
  supermarket*)

I make this salad as much for the oily joy on the plate as for the scallops themselves; as soon as you make it, you'll get what I mean. The crunchy corn is a revelation, and if you skip it, you'd be missing out!

SUBS Ⓥ Ⓥ Use paprika instead of 'nduja and oyster mushrooms instead of scallops; swap the butter for olive oil for vegans.

GET AHEAD Make the dressing in advance. Grill the corn cobs and cut off the kernels up to 3 hours in advance, then leave in the dressing.

1] Preheat the grill to high. Bring a wide pan of water to the boil. Add the corn cobs and boil for 5 minutes, remove with tongs and pat dry with kitchen paper. Place on a baking tray, brush with a little of the butter and grill for 10–15 minutes, turning frequently, until they're charred on all sides.

2] Whisk up the dressing in a large mixing bowl. Stand each corn cob in turn upright and use a knife to slide down the cob and cut the kernels off. Add to the dressing.

3] Heat a frying pan over a medium-high heat. Peel and finely slice the garlic. Add the 'nduja or chorizo and garlic to the frying pan – *if using chorizo, add a tiny splash of olive oil*. Fry for 2–3 minutes until the 'nduja is turning a slightly darker red, then add to the bowl of dressing and corn.

4] Halve the tomatoes and add to the bowl. Pull the herb leaves from the stems, roughly chop most of them and add to the bowl. Season well with salt and pepper. Toss, then transfer the salad to a platter.

5] Wipe out the frying pan, then heat over a high heat and add the remaining butter. Season the scallops. Once the butter is foaming, add the scallops and cook for 2 minutes, turn them over and cook for 1 minute on the other side. Transfer to the platter, snuggling them into the salad. Top with the remaining herbs and crunchy corn. Finish with a crack of black pepper. Slice the lime into wedges and serve on the side.

Charred Onion & Pomegranate

SERVES 4
TIME 25 mins
VIBE Easy-peasy

NICE ON THE SIDE
Kebabs and flatbreads

SALAD PARTY?
Serve with Spiced Aubergine
& Lentil (*see* page 111) and/or
Za'atar Fattoush (*see* page 95)

4 white onions
2 tablespoons olive oil
1 teaspoon sumac
1 teaspoon Aleppo pepper (pul
    biber) or other chilli flakes
handful of mint leaves
handful of flat leaf parsley
    leaves
50g (1¾oz) pomegranate seeds
salt

DRESSING
Lemon & Olive Oil (*see*
    page 16), plus 2 tablespoons
    pomegranate molasses

TOPPERS
a pinch of the Aleppo pepper
    (pul biber) or other chilli
    flakes (*see* above)

Whenever I have Turkish food, I order the onion salad – and you should do likewise, as it's usually as good, if not better, than the rest of the meal. This is based on all the great ones that I've eaten. I haven't cooked it over charcoal here just so that more people can cook it easily. But it would be a beaut if you were to place the onion halves over a hot barbecue and char until softened, then proceed with the recipe!

GET AHEAD Make the dressing in advance.

1] Preheat the oven to 240°C/220°C fan/475°F/Gas Mark 9. Peel and quarter the onions, then put into a roasting tray, drizzle with the oil and toss to coat. Season generously with salt and roast for 15-20 minutes, depending on the size of your onions – *you want them to be soft and sweet but not mushy*. Then turn on the grill to high and grill for 6–8 minutes, turning halfway, until they're charred.

2] Meanwhile, whisk up the dressing including the pomegranate molasses in a large mixing bowl, then whisk in the sumac and most of the Aleppo pepper or chilli flakes. Finely chop the herbs and add to the bowl, then add the pomegranate seeds and toss to combine.

3] Use a fork to separate the charred onions and space the petals out on a serving plate. Drizzle with the dressing, then sprinkle with the remaining Aleppo pepper or chilli flakes.

Lamb Meatballs with Charred Courgettes

SERVES 4
TIME 50 mins
VIBE Showing off a little

NICE ON THE SIDE
Fresh green salad or pitta breads

SALAD PARTY?
Serve with The Ultimate Green Salad (*see* page 30) and/or Triple Tomato (*see* page 44)

500g (1lb 2oz) minced lamb – *with a high percentage of fat*
1 egg
1 onion
1 garlic cloves
1 teaspoon fennel seeds
1 teaspoon dried oregano
3 courgettes
olive oil
1 small bunch (about 30g/1oz) mint
1 small bunch (about 30g/1oz) dill
250g (9oz) thick Greek yogurt
salt and pepper

DRESSING
Green Sauce (*see* page 17), plus 2 tablespoons pickled sliced jalapeños (for homemade *see* page 23)

TOPPERS
50g (1¾oz) blanched hazelnuts or 30g (1oz) pine nuts (optional)
a few of the herbs (*see* above)

Meatballs can be a salad! To prove that point, here they are teamed with grilled courgettes, piled on a bed of thick creamy yogurt and drizzled with a herby/chilli-spiked sauce. It'd be a real shame not to serve this with flatbread to mop the plate with.

SUBS Ⓥ Swap the minced lamb for plant-based mince. Ⓥ Use plant-based mince with a vegan egg replacer and a vegan yogurt – I use coconut yogurt.

GET AHEAD Make the dressing in advance, but be aware that it'll lose its colour over time.

1] Roast the hazelnuts or pine nuts (*see* page 22), if using.

2] Line a baking tray with nonstick baking paper. Put the minced lamb in a large bowl. Crack in the egg. Peel and finely chop the onion and garlic, then add to the bowl along with the fennel seeds and dried oregano. Season generously with salt and pepper. Use your hands to mix together well, then roll into 20 balls and place them on the lined tray. Set aside in the refrigerator for at least 30 minutes to firm up while you prepare the rest of the salad.

3] Blitz up the green sauce ingredients, then add the pickled jalapeños and blitz again. Set aside.

4] Preheat the oven to 200°C/180°C fan/400°F/Gas Mark 6. Cut the courgettes into 2cm (¾-inch) chunks or slices, add to a mixing large bowl along with 2 tablespoons olive oil and toss to coat. Heat a griddle pan or large frying pan (*or put them on a hot barbecue!*) over a high heat, and once hot, add the courgettes and cook for 4 minutes on each side until they're charred and totally collapsed –

you may have to do this in 2 batches. Return to the bowl and add 2 tablespoons of the dressing. Pull the herb leaves from the stems, roughly chop and add most of them to the bowl, then toss to combine.

5] Drizzle the meatballs with a little olive oil and bake for 10 minutes until they look set.

6] Spread the yogurt across the base of a large platter and top with the grilled courgettes and herbs.

7] Remove the tray from the oven and place a frying pan over a medium-high heat. Add the meatballs along with a splash of olive oil and fry for 5 minutes, tossing constantly to turn them an even brown. Pile on top of the courgettes. Finish with the remaining dressing, the roasted hazelnuts or pine nuts, if using, and the remaining herbs.

Charred Lettuce

SERVES 4
TIME 35 mins
VIBE Not too tricky

NICE ON THE SIDE
Barbecued chicken

SALAD PARTY?
Serve with Grilled Greek (*see* page 157) and/or Red Pepper & Bavette (*see* pages 159–161)

1 large (or 2 small) courgette

1 lemon

½ small bunch (about 15g/½oz) dill

½ small bunch (about 15g/½oz) flat leaf parsley

4 Gem lettuces

3–4 tablespoons olive oil

250g (9oz) asparagus spears

300g (10½oz) green beans

salt and pepper

DRESSING

Caesar (*see* page 18) or Yogurt (*see* page 16)

TOPPERS

50g (1¾oz) nuts – *I used almonds* – or 30g (1oz) pumpkin seeds

30g (1oz) Parmesan cheese

Charred lettuce – take a moment to get your head round that. But once you have, you'll not regret giving it a go. It's also the perfect excuse to drench a load of delicious charred greens in Caesar dressing.

SUBS Ⓥ Use the yogurt dressing and omit the Parmesan topper. Ⓥ Use the yogurt dressing but with vegan yogurt and maple syrup instead of the honey, and omit the Parmesan topper.

GET AHEAD Make the dressing and roast the nuts or toast the seeds in advance.

1] If using a charcoal barbecue, light the barbecue, then wait until it's no longer flaming and the coals are white. Make the dressing. Roast the nuts or toast the pumpkin seeds (*see* page 22).

2] Finely slice the courgette and put in a mixing bowl. Finely grate in the zest of the lemon and squeeze in the juice. Pull the herb leaves from the stems, roughly chop and add to the bowl. Season with salt and pepper and toss to combine.

3] Slice the lettuces in half vertically – *if they look at all dirty, wash in iced water and spin to dry* – and drizzle a little of the oil over the cut sides. Put the asparagus and green beans in another mixing bowl with the remaining oil and toss to coat, then season generously. If not using a charcoal barbecue, heat a griddle pan or frying pan over a high heat. Place the lettuce halves, cut-side down, on the barbecue or hot pan and char for about 5–7 minutes until collapsing. Transfer them to a platter.

4] Add the asparagus and beans to the barbecue or pan and cook for 8–10 minutes, turning regularly, until charred and softened – *the cooking time will be less if you're using a barbecue*. Transfer to the platter. Top with the lemony courgette slices, tucking them into the charred veg. Drizzle with the dressing, then top with the roasted nuts or toasted seeds and use a peeler to shave over the Parmesan.

Cabbage & Anchovy

SERVES 4
TIME 45 mins
VIBE Easy-peasy

NICE ON THE SIDE
Grilled chicken or barbecued fish

SALAD PARTY?
Serve with Tabbouleh
(*see* page 39) and/or Triple
Tomato (*see* page 44)

2 Hispi cabbages
olive oil
salt and pepper

DRESSING

Anchovy & Lemon (*see* page
19), plus 3 tablespoons capers

TOPPERS

50g (1¾oz) Toasted
Breadcrumbs (*see* page 25)
or 30g (1oz) pine nuts
30g (1oz) Parmesan cheese

The key to making this work is to ensure that your cabbage is really well cooked, so if you're using a large cabbage and it still feels firm after the allotted time, don't be afraid to keep on cooking it. It's a great dish for serving alongside barbecued meats, or serve it over nutty grains if you want to make it a bit more substantial.

SUBS Ⓥ Ⓥ Swap the dressing for Green Sauce (*see* page 17) and omit the Parmesan topper.

GET AHEAD Make the dressing in advance.

1] If using a charcoal barbecue, light the barbecue, then wait until it's no longer flaming and the coals are white. If not using a charcoal barbecue, preheat the oven to 200°C/180°C fan/400°F/Gas Mark 6. Make the toasted breadcrumbs, or roast the pine nuts (*see* page 22).

2] Remove and discard the outer leaves from the cabbages, then slice each through the core into 4 wedges. Place the wedges on a baking tray, drizzle with olive oil and season generously with salt and pepper.

3] If using a barbecue, transfer the wedges to the barbecue and grill for 20–25 minutes, turning them regularly with tongs, until they're cooked all the way through, charred and totally collapsed.

4] If not using a charcoal barbecue, heat a frying pan over a high heat, add the wedges and cook for 5 minutes on each side. Return to the baking tray and bake for 15–20 minutes, or until totally soft – *if your Hispis are large they may need longer in the oven*. Whisk up the dressing, add the capers and set aside.

5] Use tongs to transfer the wedges to a platter. Pour over the dressing, top with the toasted breadcrumbs or roasted pine nuts and use a peeler to shave over the Parmesan.

Grilled Greek

SERVES 4
TIME 20 mins
VIBE Easy-peasy

NICE ON THE SIDE
Filo pies, whole baked fish or oregano chicken

SALAD PARTY?
Serve with Shaved Fennel & Orzo (page 47) and Lamb Meatballs with Charred Courgettes (page 150)

900g (2lb) tomatoes
2 cucumbers
½ red onion
2 × 200g (7oz) packets of feta cheese
4 thyme sprigs
2 tablespoons olive oil
2 teaspoons clear honey
180g (6¼oz) pitted kalamata olives
2 teaspoons dried oregano
salt and pepper
Pitta Chips (see page 25) or pitta breads, to serve (optional)

DRESSING
Lemon & Olive Oil (see page 16)

TOPPERS
pinch of dried oregano
handful of mint leaves

I strongly advise serving this with toasted pittas because spreading the charred feta across a wedge and topping it with the toms and cucumbers is a joy I'd so hate you to miss out on.

SUBS VE Use vegan feta-style 'cheese' or firm tofu and swap the honey for maple syrup.

GET AHEAD Make the pitta chips, if using, and dressing in advance.

1] Slice the tomatoes and cucumbers into chunky wedges. Put in a large mixing bowl along with a big pinch of salt, toss gently and set aside. Make the pitta chips, if using.

2] Preheat the grill to high. Whisk up the dressing in a mixing bowl. Peel and finely slice the red onion, then add to the dressing and set aside.

3] Line a baking tray with foil and place on the blocks of feta. Top each with 2 thyme sprigs, drizzle with the oil and honey and season with a little black pepper. Slide under the grill and grill for 5–7 minutes until the feta is softened and golden on top. Remove and set aside to cool a little. Toast the pitta breads, if using.

4] Drain the tomatoes and cucumbers – *salting them in this way maximizes their flavour* – then return to the bowl. Add the dressing and red onion along with the olives and the 2 teaspoons dried oregano. Toss well, taste and season.

5] Transfer to a platter or bowls. Top with the feta, either breaking it up or slicing each block in half diagonally and adding it in whole pieces. Finish with an extra pinch of dried oregano, the mint leaves and a crack of black pepper. *Alternatively, serve the feta on the side for people to break into as they eat.* Serve with the pitta chips or toasted pittas.

Courgette & Giant Couscous

SERVES 4
TIME 30 mins
VIBE Easy-peasy

NICE ON THE SIDE
Whole baked fish or barbecued meats

SALAD PARTY?
Serve with Grilled Greek (*see* page 157) and/or Red Pepper & Bavette (*see* pages 159–161)

½ onion or 1 banana shallot

4 courgettes

2 tablespoons olive oil

1 lemon

2 garlic cloves

1 tablespoon fennel seeds

250g (9oz) giant couscous

2 teaspoons dried oregano

½ small bunch (about 15g/½oz) tarragon

½ small bunch (about 15g/½oz) flat leaf parsley

salt and pepper

DRESSING

Honey & Mustard (*see* page 16), plus 1 extra tablespoon vinegar

TOPPERS

30g (1oz) sunflower seeds (optional)

30g (1oz) feta or Parmesan cheese

This salad will work with any kind of small pasta shape (just adjust the cooking time accordingly).

SUBS **V** Use feta rather than Parmesan as a topper. **VE** Swap the honey in the dressing for sugar or maple syrup and omit the cheese.

GET AHEAD Make the dressing and, if using, toast the sunflower seeds in advance. Cook and rinse the giant couscous up to 2 days in advance, then toss in a little olive oil and store in an airtight container in the refrigerator.

1] Whisk up the dressing including the extra vinegar in a large serving bowl. Peel and finely slice the onion or shallot, add to the dressing and stir well. Toast the sunflower seeds, if using (*see* page 22).

2] Preheat the grill to its highest setting. Line a large baking tray with foil. Cut the courgettes into 3cm (1¼-inch) chunks. Spread out on the lined tray, drizzle with 1 tablespoon of the oil and season well. Halve the lemon and add the halves, flesh-side up, to the tray. Grill for 15 minutes until the courgettes are charred and collapsing and the lemon flesh is charred – *you may have to do this in 2 batches.*

3] Meanwhile, peel and finely slice the garlic. Heat the remaining oil in a saucepan over a medium heat, add the garlic and fennel seeds and toast for 2 minutes. Transfer to the bowl of dressing. Cook the couscous according to the packet instructions then drain and rinse with cold water until completely cooled, then drain well.

4] Transfer the couscous to the serving bowl. Add the dried oregano. Pull the herb leaves from the stems and add to the bowl along with the charred courgettes. Toss, taste and season. Top with the crumbled feta or shaved Parmesan along with the toasted sunflower seeds, if using, and serve with the charred lemons for squeezing over at the table.

Red Pepper & Bavette

SERVES 4
TIME 30 mins
VIBE Showing off

NICE ON THE SIDE
Tacos or nachos

SALAD PARTY?
Serve with The Ultimate Green Salad
(see page 30) and/or Courgette &
Giant Couscous (see page 158)

1½ teaspoons smoked paprika

1½ teaspoons ground coriander

2 garlic cloves

750–1kg (1lb 10oz–2lb 4oz)
bavette steak (about 3–4
steaks)

450g (1lb) jar of roasted red
peppers (about 350g/12oz
drained weight)

3 tablespoons pickled sliced
jalapeños (see page 23 for
homemade)

1 small bunch (about 30g/1oz)
flat leaf parsley

100g (3½oz) rocket

2 limes

2 tablespoons olive oil

½ red onion

150g (5½oz) feta cheese

2–3 avocados

salt and pepper

corn tortillas, to serve (optional)

DRESSING

Honey & Mustard (see page
16), plus 1 extra tablespoon
of honey

TOPPERS

50g (1¾oz) pumpkin seeds

Maybe this is more of a DIY taco station than a typical salad, but
I won't tell if you won't. For me, it's the perfect salad, as it covers all
your bases: juicy meat, fresh leaves, creamy avo and some red
peppers (you might want to make extra for snacking on). The corn
tortillas are optional, but a salad that can be piled into a tortilla is a
salad that everyone can get on board with.

SUBS Ⓥ Ⓥ Swap the steak for fried firm tofu, and swap the honey
in the dressing for sugar or maple syrup for vegans. Omit the feta.

GET AHEAD Toast the pumpkin seeds and make the dressing in
advance. Marinate the steak up to 24 hours in advance.

1] Toast the pumpkin seeds (see page 22). Meanwhile, whisk up
the dressing in a mixing bowl. Add the smoked paprika and ground
coriander, then peel and finely grate or crush in the garlic and mix
well. Rub half of the dressing over the steaks and set aside.

2] If using a charcoal barbecue, light the barbecue, then wait until
it's no longer flaming and the coals are white. If not using a charcoal
barbecue, heat a frying pan over a high heat. Add the steaks to
the barbecue or hot pan and cook for 2–3 minutes on each side
until nicely dark on the outside but rare inside. Set aside on a
chopping board to rest. Take the pan, if using, off the heat – *but
don't pour any of the juices away!*

3] Drain the roasted red peppers and roughly slice, then add to
the remaining dressing. Finely chop the pickled jalapeños. Pull the
parsley leaves from the stems, finely chop half of them and add to the
bowl. Toss and season well with salt and pepper. If you used a pan to
cook the steaks, add the red pepper and jalapeño mixture to the pan,
tossing in the steak juices, then leave to sit while you make the rest of
the salad.

4] Put the rocket into a large mixing bowl, add the juice of 1 of the limes and the oil. Slice the remaining lime into wedges. Peel and finely slice the red onion, then add to the bowl along with the remaining parsley leaves. Add most of the toasted pumpkin seeds, then toss well. Add the feta, crumbling it into chunks with your hands. Toss again gently, then transfer to a corner of a platter.

5] Halve each avocado and remove the stone, then peel and slice into wedges. Pile beside the salad.

6] Slice the steak and pile on to the other side of a platter. Top with the red pepper and jalapeño mixture, snuggling it all in among the steak slices. Scatter with the remaining pumpkin seeds and serve with the lime wedges. I like to serve this with corn tortillas, quickly chucked on to the barbecue or into the hot pan to char just before serving, so that people can turn this mega salad into mega tacos!

Creamy

'Caesar dressing is up there, for me, with
one of the best things in the food world.
A big claim I know, but I stand by it. These
salads are the ones that go heavy on creamy
dressings, such as the Caesar, or yogurt
dressing. They're for those times that only
a salad truly bathing in dressing will hit
the spot.'

Caesar

SERVES 4
TIME 20 mins
VIBE Not too tricky

NICE ON THE SIDE
Roast or barbecued chicken

SALAD PARTY?
Serve with Triple Tomato
(*see* page 44) and/or Potato Salad:
The Crispy One (*see* page 177)

Croutons (see page 23)
4 chicken breasts (optional)
olive oil
4 Romaine hearts
salt and pepper

DRESSING
Caesar or Cheat's Caesar
   (*see* page 18)

TOPPERS
30g (1oz) Parmesan cheese

I couldn't write a salad book without a Caesar (or two). This is the more traditional guy, spiked with croutons and featuring leaves that need a knife and fork. The garlic in the dressing is optional – I'm not a fan of raw garlic and so you are more than welcome to skip it too. Shout out to Molly Baz, Caesar extraordinaire, for constant Caesar inspiration.

SUBS Ⓥ Omit the chicken, and omit the anchovies and use a vegetarian hard cheese in the dressings and for topping. Ⓥᴱ Omit the chicken and use the cheat's Caesar dressing with vegan mayonnaise and Parmesan-style 'cheese' (also use for topping), omitting the anchovies.

GET AHEAD Make the croutons and dressing in advance.

1] Make the croutons. Meanwhile, make the dressing.

2] If using chicken, rub the breasts with a little olive oil and season well with salt and pepper. Set a frying pan over a medium-high. Once hot, add the chicken and cook for 4–5 minutes on each side. Remove from the pan and set aside to rest for 10 minutes.

3] Separate the leaves of the lettuce hearts – *if they look at all dirty, wash in iced water and spin to dry* – and add to a large bowl. Add the dressing and toss until the leaves are all well coated. Add the croutons. If using chicken, slice and add to the salad. Toss again, then transfer to a platter. Grate over the Parmesan and finish with a big crack of black pepper.

Creamy Pasta

SERVES 4
TIME 30 mins
VIBE Easy-peasy

NICE ON THE SIDE
Big green salad and garlic bread

SALAD PARTY?
Serve with The Ultimate Green Salad (*see* page 30) and/or Cabbage & Anchovy (*see* page 154)

100g (3½oz) pine nuts
300g (10½oz) farfalle or other small pasta shape of choice
200g (7oz) frozen peas
1 lemon
4 tablespoons capers
360g (12¾oz) hot-smoked salmon
1 small bunch (about 30g/1oz) dill
salt and pepper

DRESSING
Yogurt (*see* page 16), swapping 3 tablespoons of the yogurt for mayonnaise

TOPPERS
a little of the dill (*see* above)
a few of the pine nuts (*see* above)

Yes, this would be nice warm, but who doesn't love a big ol' creamy pasta salad?

SUBS **V** Swap the salmon for chunks of feta cheese. **VE** Swap the salmon for roasted veggies, and use vegan yogurt and mayonnaise and maple syrup instead of honey in the dressing.

GET AHEAD Cook and rinse the pasta up to 2 days in advance, then toss in a little olive oil and store in an airtight container in the refrigerator. Make the dressing in advance.

1] Roast the pine nuts (*see* page 22).

2] Bring a large pan of salted water to the boil, add the pasta and cook according to the packet instructions.

3] Meanwhile, mix up the dressing in a large mixing bowl. Add the frozen peas – *they will defrost when everything gets mixed together.* Then finely grate in the zest of the lemon and squeeze in the juice, add the capers and stir well.

4] Drain the pasta and rinse with cold water until completely cooled, then drain well. Add to the mixing bowl and stir well, then flake in the salmon. Pull the dill leaves from the stems, roughly chop and add most to the bowl along with most of the roasted pine nuts. Gently toss, then taste and season generously with salt and pepper. Top with the remaining dill and pine nuts and tip onto a large platter or into bowls.

Creamy Avocado

NICE ON THE SIDE
I'd serve this as a perfect light lunch. Add some feta cheese for an extra flavour punch.

SALAD PARTY?
I'd keep this for a low-key lunch rather than a big salad party!

200g (7oz) quinoa
250g (9oz) pouch of
    ready-cooked Puy lentils
30g (1oz) mixed soft herbs –
    I used coriander and
    flat leaf parsley
juice of 1 lemon (about
    2 tablespoons)
280g (10oz) firm tofu
2 tablespoons olive oil
200g (7oz) edamame beans
200g (7oz) cherry tomatoes
150g (5½oz) radishes
3 carrots
salt and pepper

DRESSING
Vegan Avo (*see page 17*)

TOPPERS
a few of the herbs (*see above*)
2 tablespoons poppy seeds

Here's the thing, this is a little like one of those bowls that you get in health-food shops, and honestly, I've always seen them as a bit of an excuse for a salad, but I decided to turn the concept on its head. This IS a grain bowl, yes, but it's punchy and crunchy and covered in a creamy drizzle, so it really puts those portion-controlled bowls to shame.

GET AHEAD Cook and rinse the quinoa up to 2 days in advance, then store in an airtight container in the refrigerator. Make the dressing in advance, but be aware that it'll lose its colour over time.

1] Bring a pan of salted water to the boil, add the quinoa and cook for 10–15 minutes until the grains have opened up. Drain and rinse with cold water until completely cooled, then drain well and put in a large mixing bowl.

2] Blitz up the vegan avo dressing, then loosen with a little water to the consistency of double cream.

3] Add the lentils to the quinoa. Pull the herb leaves from the stems and roughly chop, then add most of them to the bowl. Add the lemon juice and 2 tablespoons of the dressing, and season well with salt and pepper. Toss to combine, then spoon into bowls.

4] Slice the tofu into 4cm (1½-inch) lengths and season. Heat the oil in a frying pan over a medium-high heat, add the tofu and fry for 3 minutes on each side until crisp. Transfer to the bowls.

5] Divide the edamame between the bowls. Halve the tomatoes and divide them between the bowls. Finely slice the radishes and do the same. Peel the carrots, then use the peeler to peel them into ribbons. Divide between the bowls. Drizzle the salads with the dressing and sprinkle with the remaining herbs and poppy seeds.

Egg, Bacon & Gem Lettuce

SERVES 4
TIME 45 mins
VIBE Easy-peasy

NICE ON THE SIDE
Bread, just in case you actually
want to make it into a sandwich!

SALAD PARTY?
Serve with Frozen Pea, Mint
& Cucumber (page 29) and/or
Ham 'n' Melon (page 53)

450g (1lb) chunky tomatoes
6 eggs
12 streaky bacon rashers
3 Gem lettuces
juice of ½ lemon (about
    1 tablespoon)
2 tablespoons olive oil
½ small bunch (about 15g/½oz)
    chives
salt and pepper

DRESSING
Caesar or Cheat's Caesar (*see*
    page 18), omitting
    the Parmesan

TOPPERS
Serve with slices of
    sourdough toast

A glorified BLT you may say. Yeah maybe, but let's call it a salad and
be really happy about that.

SUBS 🅥 Swap the bacon for plant-based bacon or fried aubergine
slices and omit the anchovies in the dressing. 🆅🅔 As for 🅥 but use
the cheat's Caesar dressing with vegan mayonnaise and omit the
anchovies; omit the eggs.

GET AHEAD Make the dressing in advance. Boil the eggs up to
3 days in advance, cool and store in an airtight container in the
refrigerator.

1] Slice the tomatoes into chunky wedges, Put in a large mixing bowl
with a big pinch of salt and set aside while you make the rest of the
salad. Meanwhile, preheat the grill to high and line a baking tray with foil.
Bring a pan of water to the boil. Make the dressing.

2] Drop the eggs into the boiling water, reduce the heat a little and
cook for 6–8 minutes, then use a spoon or tongs to remove the eggs
and rinse until cool.

3] While the eggs are cooking, lay the bacon rashers on the lined
tray and grill for 4 minutes, then turn the pieces over and grill for
another 4 minutes – *they should be super-crispy but not burned*.
Set aside on kitchen paper.

4] Drain the tomatoes and return to the bowl. Separate the leaves of the
lettuces and wash, then add to the mixing bowl with the tomatoes, then
add the lemon juice and oil. Use scissors to snip most of the chives into
the bowl. Season with salt and pepper and toss well. Transfer to a platter.

5] Roughly break up the bacon, shell and halve the eggs, then add
both to the platter. Drizzle everything with the dressing. Finish with the
remaining chives and black pepper. Serve with sourdough toast.

Brown Butter Greens

SERVES 4
TIME 40 mins
VIBE Feeling a little more fancy

NICE ON THE SIDE
Warm crusty bread or barbecued chicken

SALAD PARTY?
Serve with Triple Tomato (*see page 44*) or Spicy Pasta (*see page 89*)

200g (7oz) asparagus spears
400g (14oz) Tenderstem broccoli
250g (9oz) thick Greek yogurt
1 lemon
½ tablespoon olive oil
salt and pepper

MINTY BROWN BUTTER

60g (2¼oz) salted butter
1 small bunch (about 30g/1oz) mint

TOPPERS

4 each of the broccoli spears and asparagus spears, about 100g (3½oz) in total (*see above*)
60g (2¼oz) almonds

So, you're having a barbecue and you need to show off with something that really is better than the other things getting grilled. That's when this salad comes into its own.

SUBS Ⓥ Use coconut yogurt and swap the butter for olive oil but simply heat it until it shimmers, then add the chopped mint.

GET AHEAD Make the yogurt, pickled veg and minty brown butter up to 24 hours in advance, then store in airtight containers in the refrigerator. Warm the minty brown butter again when assembling.

1] Snap the woody ends off the asparagus. Finely slice 4 of the asparagus spears and 4 of the broccoli spears, then pickle (*see* page 23). Roast the almonds (*see* page 22), then roughly chop.

2] To make the minty brown butter, put the butter in a frying pan and place over a medium heat. Once the butter has melted, keep whisking it as it foams and then turns brown and smells like nuts – about 4 minutes, then remove from the heat. Finely chop the mint leaves and add to the butter – *be careful, as it will fizz up a bit!* Set aside. If not using a charcoal barbecue, preheat the grill to high.

3] Put the yogurt in a bowl, finely grate in the zest of the lemon, squeeze in the juice of one half and mix. Taste and season well, then add a little lemon juice to taste. Spread across the base of a large platter.

4] Lay the remaining broccoli and asparagus on a baking tray, drizzle with the oil and season generously. Slide under the grill and cook, turning regularly, for about 10 minutes until charred, or transfer to the barbecue to char, turning regularly – *the cooking time will be less if you're using a barbecue.*

5] Pile the broccoli and asparagus on top of the yogurt and drizzle with the minty brown butter. Top with the pickled veg and roasted almonds.

Prawn Cocktail

SERVES 4
TIME 20 mins
VIBE Feeling a little more fancy

NICE ON THE SIDE
Chilled white wine

SALAD PARTY?
Serve with Courgette & White Bean (*see* page 28) and/or Shaved Fennel & Orzo (*see* page 47)

juice of 1 lemon (about 2 tablespoons)
500g (1lb 2oz) large raw peeled prawns
1 large cucumber
2 Gem lettuces
3 tablespoons capers
1 small bunch (about 30g/1oz) dill and/or flat leaf parsley
2 tablespoons mayonnaise
1 tablespoon Sriracha or tomato ketchup
salt and pepper

DRESSING
Lemon & Olive Oil (*see* page 16)

TOPPERS
50g (1¾oz) Toasted Breadcrumbs with chilli powder (*see* page 25) or a pinch of chilli flakes

If you don't like a prawn salad, maybe flick to the next page. I love it so much that I made it into a full-on meal here. Apply a little dressing to serve, then dish up the rest on the side ready for everyone to soak their portions with!

SUBS Ⓥ Swap the prawns for wedges of feta cheese. ⓋⒼ Swap the prawns for tempeh and use vegan mayonnaise.

GET AHEAD Cook the prawns, drain and dry up to 24 hours in advance, then store in an airtight container in the refrigerator. Make the dressing and the dressing and mayo mixture up to a week in advance.

1] Bring a large pan of water to the boil. Fill a bowl with iced water. Season the pan of water generously with salt and add the lemon juice. Drop the prawns into the boiling water and cook for 30–60 seconds, depending on their size, until they turn pink. Use a slotted spoon to quickly transfer them into the iced water. Once cooled, drain and pat dry on kitchen paper, cover and set aside in the refrigerator until ready to assemble the salad.

2] Make the toasted breadcrumbs, if using. Whisk up the dressing.

3] Cut the cucumber in half lengthways, then slice into half moons and put in a large mixing bowl. Slice the lettuces into quarters through the base – *if they look at all dirty, wash in iced water and spin to dry* – then add to the bowl along with the capers. Pull the herb leaves from the stems and add most of them to the bowl. Add half of the dressing and season with salt and pepper. Gently toss, then transfer to a large plate. Top with the prawns.

4] Mix the remaining dressing with the mayo and Sriracha or ketchup. Taste and season, then drizzle over the salad. Top with the remaining herb leaves and the toasted breadcrumbs or chilli flakes.

The Best Salad is a Potato Salad:
The Crispy One

SERVES 4
TIME 1 hour
VIBE Easy-peasy

NICE ON THE SIDE
Fish, chicken and pretty much anything non-carb based. Did I mention that I love potato salad?

SALAD PARTY?
Serve with the Lamb Meatballs with Charred Courgettes (page 150) and/ or Chop Chop Feta (page 185)

1kg (2lb 4oz) baby potatoes
80g (2¾oz) diced pancetta
2–3 tablespoons olive oil
1 small bunch (about 100g/3½oz) spring onions
75g (2¾oz) capers
½ small bunch (about 15g/½oz) chives
salt and pepper

DRESSING
Yogurt (see page 16), swapping 75g (2¾oz) of the yogurt for 75g (2¾oz) mayonnaise

I'm obsessed with potato salads. They are the ultimate crowd-pleaser, so everyone loves the person that makes a good version. Here are two that use the same ingredients but produce very different results. This crispy one is a potential favourite of the whole book, you know a salad is good when you wake up from a party and people ask for the recipe. I hope you get to make these beauties and experience the exact same thing.

SUBS **V** Omit the pancetta. **VE** Omit the pancetta, and use vegan yogurt and mayonnaise and maple syrup instead of honey in the dressing.

GET AHEAD Boil the potatoes up to 2 days in advance, rinse until cooled and drain, then store in an airtight container in the refrigerator. Crush and then roast and grill from cold – they may take a little longer. Make the dressing in advance.

1] Preheat the oven to 220°C/200°C fan/425°F/Gas Mark 7. Scrub the potatoes if dirty, then put them into a large saucepan, cover with water and add a big pinch of salt. Place over a high heat, bring to the boil and cook for 15–20 minutes, depending on size, or until a knife slides through them without any resistance. *Don't let them go too far, as you don't want to be serving mashed potatoes!*

2] Meanwhile, line a plate with kitchen paper. Heat a large frying pan over a medium-high heat, add the pancetta along with a splash of the oil and fry for 5–7 minutes until crispy. Transfer to the lined plate to drain. Reserve the fat.

3] Line a baking tray with foil. Drain the potatoes well, then add to the tray and use a fork or spatula to gently press them down on them until the skin bursts and they flatten. Drizzle with the reserved pancetta fat plus 1–2 tablespoons of the olive oil and season well with salt and pepper. Roast for 20–30 minutes. Turn on the grill to high, slide the potatoes under the grill and cook for another 10 minutes until crispy.

4] While the potatoes are crisping up, mix up the dressing. Remove the outer layers from the spring onions.

5] Transfer the potatoes to a platter. Put the spring onions on the baking tray, drizzle with the remaining oil and season. Grill for 10 minutes until they're charred and softened, then snuggle on to the platter with the potatoes.

6] Drizzle with the dressing, sprinkle with the capers and crispy pancetta and use scissors to finely snip the chives over the top.

The Best Salad Is a Potato Salad:
The Boiled One

SERVES 4
TIME 25 mins
VIBE Easy-peasy

NICE ON THE SIDE
Barbecued meats or fish

SALAD PARTY?
Serve with Grilled Greek (*see* page 157) and/or Red Pepper & Bavette (*see* page 159–161)

1kg (2lb 4oz) baby potatoes
80g (2¾oz) diced pancetta
2 tablespoons olive oil
1 small bunch (about 100g/3½oz) spring onions
½ small bunch (about 15g/½oz) chives
75g (2¾oz) capers

DRESSING
Yogurt (*see* page 16), swapping 75g (2¾oz) of the yogurt for 75g (2¾oz) mayonnaise

Using exactly the same ingredients as the crispy potato salad, but this guy looks a little more like what we imagine a potato salad to be.

SUBS Ⓥ Omit the pancetta. ⓋⒺ Omit the pancetta, and use vegan yogurt and mayonnaise and maple syrup instead of honey in the dressing.

GET AHEAD Boil and cool the potatoes up to 2 days in advance, then store in an airtight container in the refrigerator. Make the dressing in advance.

1] Scrub the potatoes if dirty, then put them into a large saucepan, cover with water and add a big pinch of salt. Place over a high heat, bring to the boil and cook for 15–20 minutes, depending on size, or until a knife slides through them without any resistance. *Don't let them go too far, as you don't want to be serving mashed potatoes!*

2] Meanwhile, line a plate with kitchen paper. Heat a large frying pan over a medium-high heat, add the pancetta along with a splash of the oil and fry for 5–7 minutes until crispy. Transfer to the lined plate to drain.

3] Mix up the dressing in a large serving bowl. Finely slice the spring onions and chives and add most to the bowl with the capers.

4] Drain and rinse the potatoes with cold water until cooled, then drain well and add to the bowl along with most of the crispy pancetta. Toss well, drizzle with the remaining olive oil and scatter with the rest of the reserved ingredients.

Cheesy

'A lot of my salads feature cheese, particularly feta and Parmesan because, let's be honest, we all have favourites don't we. These salads, however, are for when the cheese is the star. They're the salads for when you want the other ingredients to be looking at the cheese kind of wishing they were standing centre-stage.'

Pumpkin & Burrata

SERVES 4
TIME 1 hour
VIBE Showing off

NICE ON THE SIDE
Roasted pork shoulder or big hunks of sourdough bread

SALAD PARTY?
Serve with Winter Citrus (*see* page 121) and/or Cauli Wedge (*see* page 139)

1 pumpkin (about 1kg/2lb 4oz) – *I use Delica; you can use squash but it'll take a little longer to cook!*

3 red onions

2 tablespoons olive oil

60g (2¼oz) unsalted butter

1 small bunch (about 30g/1oz) sage

pinch of chilli flakes (optional)

1 lemon

60g (2¼oz) watercress

3 × 125g (4½oz) balls of burrata cheese

salt and pepper

TOPPERS

60g (2¼oz) blanched hazelnuts

lemon zest, optional

Photographed on page 182

This is the meal you cook when you can grab some fancier ingredients. it's here to make you look like the chef you know you are.

SUBS **V** Make sure your burrata is vegetarian. **VE** Omit the burrata, and swap the butter for olive oil, but be aware that it won't brown like the butter!

GET AHEAD Toast the hazelnuts in advance. Roast the pumpkin and red onions up to 24 hours in advance and store in an airtight container in the fridge. To serve, return to the oven for 5–10 minutes to reheat.

1] Roast the hazelnuts (see page 22). Increase the oven temperature (or preheat) to 220°C/200°C fan/425°F/Gas Mark 7. Cut the pumpkin in half and scoop out all the seeds, then cut into long wedges. Peel the red onions and cut into wedges. Put both on a baking tray lined with foil. Drizzle with the oil, season generously with salt and pepper and roast for about 25–30 minutes, or until the pumpkin is completely soft.

2] Meanwhile, Put the butter in a frying pan over a medium heat. Once the butter has melted, keep whisking it as it foams and then turns brown and smells like nuts – about 4 minutes. Add the sage leaves to the brown butter and cook for 2–3 minutes until crisp and dark green. Remove from the heat, add the chilli flakes, if using, and season.

3] Squeeze the juice of the lemon into a mixing bowl and add the watercress. Season and toss.

4] Transfer the pumpkin and red onion mixture to a platter. Add the watercress and distribute it among the pumpkin. Snuggle the burrata into the salad and season with salt, then drizzle everything with the crispy sage leaves and brown butter.

5] Roughly chop the hazelnuts and sprinkle on top, then finish with black pepper and the lemon zest, if using.

Chop Chop Feta

SERVES 4
TIME 20 mins
VIBE Easy-peasy

NICE ON THE SIDE
Barbecued meats or fish – I love to serve this with barbecued chicken skewers

SALAD PARTY?
Serve with Lamb Meatballs with Charred Courgettes (page 150) and Potato: The Crispy One (page 176–179)

4 plum tomatoes
75g (2¾oz) dried cranberries
1 red onion
3 celery sticks
2 Gem or Romaine lettuces
50g (1¾oz) rocket
1 small bunch (about 30g/1oz) flat leaf parsley
1 small bunch (about 30g/1oz) mint
200g (7oz) of feta cheese
salt and pepper

DRESSING
Honey & Mustard (see page 16) – *sub white balsamic for the cider or white wine vinegar if you have it*

This is as much fun to make as it is to eat, so get your biggest chopping board and get going!

SUBS Ⓥ Use vegan feta-style 'cheese', or crumble firm tofu, season with plenty of salt and a squeeze of lemon juice and use in the same way as the feta; swap the honey in the dressing for sugar or maple syrup.

GET AHEAD Salt the tomatoes up to an hour in advance. Make the dressing in advance.

1] Finely chop the tomatoes, put in a mixing bowl along with a big pinch of salt and set aside.

2] Whisk up the dressing in a large mixing bowl, then add the dried cranberries. Peel and finely chop the red onion, then add to the dressing too.

3] Now comes the fun part! Roughly slice the celery on your biggest chopping board. Separate the leaves of the lettuces – *if they look at all dirty, wash in iced water and spin to dry* – and pile on top along with the rocket. Pull the herb leaves from the stems and add on top. Start to run a knife through everything until all the ingredients are finely chopped, almost pulverizing the flavours together.

4] Drain the tomatoes, then add them to the board along with the crumbled feta and give a final run through with the knife. Add everything to the bowl with the onion, cranberries and dressing. Toss, taste and season with salt and pepper and serve immediately.

Feta & Red Pepper

SERVES 4
TIME 40 mins
VIBE Feeling a little more fancy

NICE ON THE SIDE
Warmed flatbreads or pork chops

SALAD PARTY?
Serve with Tabbouleh
(*see* page 39) or Spicy Steak
(*see* page 76)

4 roasted red peppers from
   a jar
300g (10½oz) cherry tomatoes
   on the vine
1 teaspoon paprika
2 tablespoons olive oil
2 garlic cloves
1 tablespoon red wine vinegar
2 × 200g (7oz) packets of feta
   cheese
salt and pepper

DRESSING
Zhoug (*see* page 17)

TOPPERS
50g (1¾oz) dukkah, or
   almonds, or blanched
   hazelnuts
large handful of soft herb
   leaves – *I used coriander
   and flat leaf parsley*
pinch of chilli flakes – *I used
   Aleppo pepper (pul biber)*

This book doesn't skimp on the red pepper recipes because I love them and because, once they're a little spiced and marinated, they have the power to make a salad into a real showstopper, and this guy is no exception.

SUBS 🆅🅴 Swap the feta for fried blocks of firm tofu, cut into shards, and make sure the red wine vinegar is vegan.

GET AHEAD Make the dressing, but be aware that it'll lose its colour over time, and, if using, roast the nuts in advance.

1] Preheat the oven to 220°C/200°C fan/425°F/Gas Mark 7. Tear the roasted red peppers into strips and put in a roasting tray. Add the tomatoes, sprinkle with the paprika and drizzle with the oil. Add the garlic cloves (with their skins on) to the tray. Season with salt and pepper and gently toss, then roast for 20 minutes.

2] Meanwhile, make the dressing and roast the nuts, if using (*see* page 22).

3] Remove the roasting tray from the oven and squeeze the garlic cloves from their skins into the tomatoes – *if they're too hot to handle, use the back of spoon to squish out.* Add the vinegar to the tray and gently toss. Transfer to a platter. Break the feta into large wedges and snuggle into the tomatoes and red peppers. Drizzle with the dressing and sprinkle with the herbs, chilli flakes and the roasted nuts or dukkah.

Ploughman's

SERVES 4
TIME 25 mins
VIBE Easy-peasy

NICE ON THE SIDE
Pint of beer

SALAD PARTY?
This salad is best served as an epic speedy and delicious lunch on its own

Croutons (*see* page 23), optional
100g (3½oz) mixed salad leaves
2 apples
4 celery sticks
200g (7oz) strong Cheddar cheese
8 slices of ham
80g (2¾oz) cornichons
60g (2¼oz) pickled onions (*see* page 23 for homemade)
4 tablespoons pickle of your choice (such as Branston)
2 tablespoons English mustard

DRESSING

Lemon & Olive Oil (*see* page 16), plus 1 tablespoon Worcestershire sauce

This is essentially an assembly job, but it's also a really epic salad, so who's complaining?! If you don't fancy making the croutons, you can serve this with big chunks of bread instead.

SUBS **V** Omit the ham and use extra cheese – I like to add a Brie or other soft vegetarian cheese; use vegan Worcestershire sauce in the dressing. **VE** Swap the ham for slices of fried firm tofu or tempeh, and use vegan Cheddar-style 'cheese' and Worcestershire sauce.

GET AHEAD Make the croutons and dressing in advance.

1] Make the croutons, if using.

2] Whisk up the dressing including the Worcestershire sauce in a large mixing bowl. Add the salad leaves. Quarter the apples, then cut away the core from each quarter and slice into wedges. Add to the bowl. Finely slice the celery and add to the bowl. Then add the croutons and toss everything together.

3] Slice the cheese and add to the side of a platter or plates, then arrange the ham beside it. Add the salad to the opposite side of the platter or plates. Add the cornichons and pickled onions or divide between the plates, arranging them in piles beside the cheese and ham. Finally, add the pickle and mustard to the side of the platter or a spoonful of the pickle and a swipe of mustard to each plate to serve.

Halloumi & Sesame

SERVES 4
TIME 25 mins
VIBE Easy-peasy

NICE ON THE SIDE
Green wintery salad or roasted
winter veg

SALAD PARTY?
Serve with Squash & Freekeh
(see page 134) and/or Cauli
Wedge (see page 139)

4 tablespoons sesame seeds

1 red onion

75g (2¾oz) ready-to-eat
   dried apricots

½ small bunch (about 15g/½oz)
   mint

1 lemon

pinch of chilli flakes

pinch of sugar, if needed

2 × 250g (9oz) packets of
   halloumi cheese

1 tablespoon clear honey

1 red apple

salt and pepper

DRESSING
Lemon & Olive Oil (see page 16)

TOPPERS
1 tablespoon of the sesame
   seeds (see above)

a few of the mint leaves
   (see above)

Is this a plate of cheese masquerading as a salad? Maybe, but who cares. The halloumi meets the apricot salsa and something really great happens. If you want to feel better about serving a plate of cheese and naming it a salad, add some lightly dressed rocket.

SUBS Ⓥ Swap the halloumi for slices of firm tofu, toss in a little oil and season well, then grill in the same way as the halloumi; swap the honey for maple syrup.

GET AHEAD Make the salsa up to 24 hours in advance – the mint will discolour a bit but it'll still taste delicious!

1] Toast the sesame seeds (see page 22). Whisk up the dressing in a mixing bowl. Peel and finely chop the red onion, then add to the dressing. Finely chop the apricots and add them too. Pull the mint leaves from the stems and finely chop most of them, then add to the bowl. Finely grate in the zest of the lemon and squeeze in the juice. Add the chilli flakes and 3 tablespoons of the toasted sesame seeds, then season generously with salt and pepper and toss to combine. Taste and add a pinch of sugar if it needs it.

2] Heat a griddle pan or frying pan over a high heat. Lay a piece of nonstick baking paper in the pan – *this stops the halloumi sticking to the pan as it chars*. Slice each block of halloumi into 8 rectangles. Lay the halloumi pieces in the hot griddle pan and cook for 1–2 minutes on each side until they have distinct char lines or, if you are using a frying pan, until they are blackened on each side. Drizzle with the honey in the pan.

3] Quarter the apple, then cut away the core from each quarter and cut into 5mm (¼-inch) slices. Arrange the halloumi on a large platter, alternating it with the apple slices. Top with the apricot salsa. Season with black pepper and finish with the remaining mint leaves and sesame seeds.

Artichoke & Ricotta

SERVES 4
TIME 25 mins
VIBE Easy-peasy

NICE ON THE SIDE
Warm sourdough bread or slow-cooked lamb shoulder and a big green salad

SALAD PARTY?
Serve with Fig & Feta (*see* page 62) and/or Spiced Aubergine & Lentil (*see* page 111)

75g (2¾oz) almonds
1 onion
100g (3½oz) pitted green olives
350g (12oz) chargrilled artichokes
100g (3½oz) watercress
1 small bunch (about 30g/1oz) dill
250g (9oz) ricotta cheese
1 lemon
salt and pepper

DRESSING
Honey & Mustard (*see* page 16), plus 2 teaspoons za'atar or dried thyme

TOPPERS
a few of the roasted almonds and dill leaves (*see* above)

This is a super-quick option for a fancy salad. It looks good, it tastes good and people will rave about it long after they've left.

SUBS Ⓥ Use a vegan soft 'cheese' in place of ricotta and swap the honey in the dressing for sugar or maple syrup.

GET AHEAD Roast the almonds and make the dressing in advance.

1] Roast the almonds (*see* page 22).

2] Whisk up the dressing including the za'atar or dried thyme in a large mixing bowl. Peel and finely slice the onion, then add to the bowl of dressing. Add the olives, breaking them up with your hands as you go, then add the artichokes and toss well. Add the watercress to the bowl. Pull the dill leaves from the stems and add most of them to the bowl, then roughly chop the roasted almonds and add most of them too. *Hold off tossing just yet!*

3] Put the ricotta into a mixing bowl, finely grate in the zest of the lemon and mix together. Season generously with salt and pepper, then spread across the base of a large platter. Cut the zested lemon into wedges.

4] Toss the salad, taste and season, then pile on top of the ricotta mixture. Finish with the remaining roasted almonds and dill leaves.

Blue Cheese Waldorf

SERVES 4
TIME 25 mins
VIBE Easy-peasy

NICE ON THE SIDE
Steak and chips

SALAD PARTY?
Serve with Leeks & Cannellini Beans (*see* page 125) and/or Cabbage & Anchovy (*see* page 154)

100g (3½oz) walnuts
50g (1¾oz) raisins
2 Romaine lettuces
100g (3½oz) rocket
2 red apples
100g (3½oz) red grapes
½ small bunch (about 15g/½oz) flat leaf parsley
½ small bunch (about 15g/½oz) chives
140g (5oz) Stilton cheese – *or any smelly blue cheese*
pepper

DRESSING
Honey & Mustard (*see* page 16), plus 2 tablespoons mayonnaise – *use white balsamic in place of cider or white wine vinegar if you can find it*

TOPPERS
a few of the walnuts (*see* above)
a little of the parsley (*see* above)

This recipe has been passed down by my aunt, who's a whizz at cooking and decided to add blue cheese to her Waldorf in a spark of genius. I think you'll get right on board with her take on it!

SUBS ⓋⒺ Use a vegan blue-style 'cheese', and vegan mayonnaise and sugar or maple syrup instead of honey in the dressing.

GET AHEAD Roast the walnuts and make the dressing in advance.

1] Roast the walnuts (*see* page 22).

2] Whisk up the dressing including the mayo in a large mixing bowl, then add the raisins.

3] Shred the lettuces – *if they look at all dirty, wash in iced water and spin to dry* – and add to the bowl along with the rocket, *but don't toss just yet!* Core the apples and finely slice, then add to the bowl. Halve the grapes, then add those too. Roughly chop the roasted walnuts, pull the parsley leaves from the stems and roughly chop and add most to the bowl, then finely slice the chives and add. Toss the salad well.

4] Transfer to a platter or bowls. Crumble the blue cheese over the top and finish with the remaining roasted walnuts and parsley and a crack of black pepper.

Spring Veg & Mozzarella

SERVES 4
TIME 25 mins
VIBE Easy-peasy

NICE ON THE SIDE
Barbecued chicken or meats, crusty baguette or fresh fish

SALAD PARTY?
Serve with Spicy Steak (*see* page 76) and/or Potato Salad: The Crispy One (*see* page 176–179)

300g (10½oz) asparagus spears
300g (10½oz) sugar snap peas
200g (7oz) frozen peas
2 courgettes
30g (1oz) soft herbs – *I used a mixture of flat leaf parsley, tarragon and dill*
3 × 125g (4½) balls of mozzarella cheese
1 lemon
salt and pepper

DRESSING
Green Sauce or Salsa Verde (*see* page 17), or Lemon & Olive Oil (*see* page 16)

TOPPERS
50g (1¾oz) nuts – *I used flaked almonds*

You can trade in the mozzarella for burrata here, if it takes your fancy! You can also roast the greens if you like. I love them blanched because the result is so fresh and tastes like springtime, but it's just as delicious with them charred.

SUBS 🅥 Make sure your mozzarella (or burrata) is vegetarian.
🆅🅴 Use vegan mozzarella-style 'cheese' or top with crumbled vegan feta-style 'cheese' instead.

GET AHEAD Make the dressing in advance, but be aware that it'll lose its colour over time. Boil the veg up to 2 days in advance, then keep in an airtight container in the refrigerator.

1] Toast the nuts (*see* page 22). Meanwhile, make the dressing of your choice.

2] Bring a large pan of salted water to the boil, and fill a bowl with iced water. Snap the woody ends off the asparagus, then add along with the sugar snaps to the boiling water and cook for 4 minutes. Add the peas and cook for another 30 seconds. Drain and plunge into the iced water. Once cooled, drain and set aside on kitchen paper to dry.

3] Finely slice the courgettes and put in a large mixing bowl. Pull the herb leaves from the stems and add most of them to the bowl. Add the drained veg along with half of the dressing. Finely grate the zest of the lemon into the bowl, then halve and squeeze in the juice of one half. Toss, taste and season with salt and pepper, then transfer to a platter.

4] Snuggle the mozzarella balls into the salad, then tear open and season them with a little salt. Drizzle over the remaining dressing and finish with the remaining herb leaves and roasted nuts. Add a crack of black pepper, then serve with the remaining lemon half for squeezing over if you think it needs a little more acidity.

Blue Cheese, Bacon & Celery

SERVES 4
TIME 30 mins
VIBE Easy-peasy

NICE ON THE SIDE
Steak and chips

SALAD PARTY?
Serve with Leeks & Cannellini Beans (*see page 125*)

75g (2¾oz) blanched hazelnuts
220g (7¾oz) streaky bacon rashers
4–5 celery sticks
2 heads of chicory
2 pears
160g (5¾oz) blue cheese
1 small bunch (about 30g/1oz) dill
salt and pepper

DRESSING
Lemon & Olive Oil (*see page 16*)

TOPPERS
a few of the hazelnuts (*see above*)
a few of the dill leaves (*see above*)

A wintery salad that really says that a salad doesn't have to be a plate of leaves but instead a robust mix of cheese, bacon and a suggestion of celery.

SUBS **V** Swap the bacon for plant-based bacon or crispy slices of parsnip. **VE** As for **V** plus use vegan blue-style 'cheese'.

GET AHEAD Roast the hazelnuts and make the dressing in advance.

1] Roast the hazelnuts (*see page 22*).

2] Preheat the grill to high. Line a baking tray with foil and place on the bacon. Grill for 4 minutes, then turn the rashers over and grill for another 4 minutes – *they should be super-crispy but not burned*. Set aside on kitchen paper.

3] Whisk up the dressing in a large mixing bowl. Slice the celery on the diagonal and add to the bowl. Separate the leaves of the chicory and add them too – *don't toss yet*. Slice the pears lengthways into quarters, then cut away the core from each quarter, slice and add to the bowl. Crumble the blue cheese into the bowl.

4] Chop the roasted hazelnuts. Pull the dill leaves from the stems and add most of them to the bowl along with most of the hazelnuts. Toss, taste and season well with salt and pepper. Transfer the salad to a platter, nestle in the crispy bacon and top with the remaining hazelnuts and dill leaves.

Goats' Cheese & Lentil

SERVES 4
TIME 35 mins
VIBE Easy-peasy

NICE ON THE SIDE
Baguette!

SALAD PARTY?
Serve with Raw Broccoli &
Almond (*see* page 33)

75g (2¾oz) walnuts

1 red onion

500g (1lb 2oz) asparagus
spears

2 × 250g (9oz) pouches of
ready-cooked Puy lentils

60g (2¼oz) lamb's lettuce

30g (1oz) mixed flat leaf parsley
and tarragon – *if you can't
get hold of tarragon, use only
1 small bunch (about 30g/1oz)
flat leaf parsley*

2 × 125g (4½oz) goats' cheese
logs – *be sure to get firm
goats' cheese!*

2 tablespoons clear honey

salt and pepper

DRESSING
Honey & Mustard (*see* page 16)

TOPPERS
a few of the walnuts
(*see* above)

a few of the herb leaves
(*see* above)

I tried a lot of different goats' cheese cooking techniques and this was my fave. It's gooey and indulgent, and it tastes so so great with the asparagus and lentils and sharp dressing. You'll be in love as soon as you give it a go!

SUBS 🅥 Use vegan goats'-style 'cheese' or omit and drizzle with a vegan yogurt mixed with a little lemon juice and mustard and seasoned well; swap the honey in the dressing for sugar or maple syrup.

GET AHEAD Roast the walnuts and make the dressing in advance. Boil the asparagus up to 24 hours in advance, then keep in an airtight container in the refrigerator.

1] Roast the walnuts (*see* page 22). Meanwhile, whisk up the dressing in a large mixing bowl. Peel and finely slice the red onion, then add to the dressing and set aside.

2] Bring a large pan of salted water to the boil, and fill a bowl with iced water. Snap the woody ends off the asparagus, add to the boiling water and cook for 3 minutes, then drain and plunge into the bowl of iced water. Drain well and pat dry with kitchen paper.

3] Add the lentils to the mixing bowl along with the lamb's lettuce. Pull the herb leaves from the stems and add most of them to the bowl. Roughly chop the roasted walnuts and add most of them to the bowl too. Gently toss, taste and season with salt and pepper, then transfer to bowls or a platter. Pile the asparagus on top.

4] Preheat the grill to high and line a baking tray with foil. Slice each of the goats' cheese logs into 6 rounds, then place on the lined tray. Slide under grill and grill for 2–3 minutes until golden and bubbling. Drizzle with the honey, then top each salad with 3 of the rounds or arrange them on top of the platter of salad. Sprinkle with the remaining walnuts and herb leaves.

Index

Acknowledgments

A massive, huge, gigantic thanks to all the people that made this book of my dreams a reality. Those who worked on the book with me, and those who dealt with all my various neuroses along the way.

Thanks firstly to the team at Octopus: Eleanor Maxfield, George Brooker and Yasia Williams. Thanks for really believing in what I wanted to create with this book.

Thanks to Chloe Hardwick and Daisy Shayler-Webb. You made this book what it is visually, you dealt with all of my random and sometimes unreasonable requests when it came to shooting the book. Daisy, you found the most amazing bits of treasure which have made their way into this book. Chloe, your photography and the general perfectionism that you brought to every shot is the reason that this book shines like it does. Thank you both for working over and above on this, it feels as much yours as it is mine.

Thanks to my incredible assistant Jodie Nixon, who is the hardest working gal in town, and through a combo of testing and being my right-hand woman on a super busy set, this book owes a whole lot to you! Big thanks also to Anna Lawson for testing recipes and providing me with invaluable feedback.

Thanks to my parents, family and friends for both feeding back on my recipe tests, and for dealing with me whenever I went into any kind of book meltdown. Particular shoutout to my housemate Abi James, who committed to eating salad for about six months.

Glossary

UK	US
aubergine	eggplant
baking tray	baking sheet
barbecue	grill
base	bottom
beetroot	beets
butter beans	lima beans
cavolo nero	Tuscan kale
celeriac	celery root
chickpeas	garbanzo beans
chicory	Belgian endive
chilli flakes	red pepper flakes
chopping board	cutting board
coriander	cilantro
courgette	zucchini
dill	dill weed
double cream	heavy cream
egg, medium (UK)	egg, large (US)
filo	phyllo
frying pan	skillet
griddle pan	grill pan
grill broiler (n); grill	broil (v)
hispi cabbage	cone cabbage

UK	US
Jerusalem artichokes	sunchokes
kitchen paper	paper towels
lengthways	lengthwise
mangetout	snow peas
natural yogurt	plain yogurt
nonstick baking paper	nonstick parchment paper
pepper	bell pepper
prawns	shrimp
rocket	arugula
runner beans	string beans
salad leaves	salad greens
sieve	strainer
spring greens	collard greens
spring onions	scallions
swede	rutabaga
streaky bacon rashers	bacon slices
sultanas	golden raisins
takeaway	take-out
tea towel	dish towel
Tenderstem broccoli	broccolini
tin	pan